12/10/10

MEN

ARE

BETTER

THAN

WOMEN

this book &
thought you
would enjoy its
title and humor,
Happy Birthday.

—Adam

Dick Masterson

SSE

SIMON SPOTLIGHT ENTERTAINMENT

New York London Toronto Sydney

SSE

SIMON SPOTLIGHT ENTERTAINMENT

A division of Simon & Schuster, Inc.

1230 Avenue of the Americas, New York, NY 10020

Copyright © 2008 by Dick Masterson

All rights reserved, including the right to reproduce this book or portions thereof in any form whatsoever. For information address Pocket Books Subsidiary Rights Department, 1230 Avenue of the Americas, New York, NY 10020

First Simon Spotlight Entertainment trade paperback edition April 2008

SIMON SPOTLIGHT ENTERTAINMENT and colophon are trademarks of Simon & Schuster, Inc.

For information about special discounts for bulk purchases, please contact Simon & Schuster Special Sales at 1-800-456-6798 or business@simonandschuster.com.

Manufactured in the United States of America

10 9 8 7 6 5 4 3

CIP data for this book is available from the Library of Congress.

ISBN-13: 978-1-4169-5381-4

ISBN-10: 1-4169-5381-7

To every man and woman in the world,
for all but writing this book for me

Acknowledgments

I thank my loyal readers, Nicolas Cage (for his manspirational films), the dozens of women I have had sex with, and, most especially, my editor, Jeremie Ruby-Strauss, for his manspertise in manhandling the manuscript into the mansterpiece you now hold in your hands: man hands.

Contents

For every woman who will make herself male will enter the kingdom of heaven.

—Jesus Christ, Gospel of Thomas

Female anger is the weather vane of truth.

—Dick Masterson

Introduction

This is Dick Masterson. Welcome to my book, *Men Are Better Than Women*.

First of all, let me congratulate you. You have taken the first and manliest steps of an unforgettable journey down the road of your own greatness. You may have noticed by now that you're a man. That makes you better than over half the people on earth. Those people are called women. Any women reading this are cautioned to put the book down and walk away. Also, try not to make a big deal out of it like you're some kind of woman Jesus. Jesus was a man, and no matter how outraged you are that the cutest sales guy in the office will only text message you when he's drunk at 3:00 a.m., you can't change that. Try losing a little weight and not acting so desperate. For example: Don't write back.

You women are delicate creatures and don't have the stomachs or the brains to look into the supernova of raw and uncensored man-logic that comprises this book. Your fragile woman-psyches cannot stand the depths of sophomoric intellect this book conjures on every page. Women, feel free to go broaden your horizons with healing crystals, Feng Shui wheels, or any of that other new-age monkey shit. Ever wonder why no one who anyone respects—like your father or Donald Trump—buys into that crap? Of course you don't, because you're a woman. You don't wonder about anything.

Now that all the women have fucked off, let me truly welcome you men to my book, because you're in for a treat: hours of discovering why having a penis is super awesome, and why having the opposite is super crappy. I'm talking about a vagina.

This book is about celebrating what it is to be a man. It's about celebrating our man-horsepower and our resourcefulness. Men are like Smurfs. When we get together in large numbers, we can fuck up Gargamels hundreds of times our size. Gargamels like the Hoover Dam and global warming. Men fix all kinds of shit.

This book is not only an illustration of man's awesomeness in the face of the impossible. It is also about pausing for a man-moment and reflecting on our deep and mature emotional nature—an emotional nature which is easily ten times deeper and more mature than that of women.

Men Are Better Than Women is about going out on the hunt and tearing the guts out of things just to see what they're made of. It's about inventing fire and rocket ships and mechanical Tyrannosaurus Rexes that can crush cars with their jaws. This book is unadulterated truth incarnate, and like a mighty man–mother eagle feeding its young, I am about to throw up nutrient-rich knowledge directly into your eyes.

Open wide.

—Dick

CHAPTER 1

The Only Real No-Collar Job
Is in a Dress

Since the beginning of time, men have worked their asses off without any expectation of gratitude or accolade. That's because we're men. We worked before we even invented money. Men are driven in a sick way to get the job done at any cost. It's a sickness called "competence."

If you've ever had a job, you'll have learned two things: Taxes suck (which is no surprise because women invented them), and women can't do anything.

Women fuck everything up. Women are like Febreze Fabric Refresher, except instead of getting out your toughest odors, they accidentally call their ex-boyfriend drunk and then won't stop crying for the rest of the night. Women will even fuck up a visit to a strip club. That's unfuckupable! A man couldn't fuck that up if he tried.

Women are a blight on the workforce bigger than flu season, Super Bowl sickness, and funny Internet videos combined. I, Dick Masterson, have gone out of my way to catalog the many ways men are better than women in all professions, and I have done so without thought of gratitude or accolade. I did it because, like all men, I, too, suffer from the crippling disease of competence.

DICK'S SEVEN DEADLY JOBS A WOMAN SHOULD NEVER EVER HAVE

I've often said that a penny saved is a woman fired. If you run a business, you know exactly what I'm talking about. Women can grind the gross production of a company from a mighty horn of commerce down to a little nub. That's only money, though. We men can always make more of it, or we can invent some new money maybe, like junk bonds or options or Spanish doubloons that have chocolate in them. The point is, there are some jobs in which women cost more than money. Sometimes, they cost lives.

I present my list of Seven Deadly Jobs a Woman Should Never Ever Have. If you or someone you know can put a stop to hiring women in any of these vocational fields, go ahead and throw your manly weight around.

1. Attorney

There was a time when lawyers were not hated like vermin. Do you know what happened between then and now? Women joined the practice of law.

In 1970, women made up 10 percent of first-year law students. Those were probably the "lesbians" of the day. "Lesbians" are all faking it, by the way; that's why it's in quotations. Actually, those 10 percent were more likely the daughters of smart, rich men who wanted to secure smart, rich husbands for their little princesses, so let's forget about "lesbians" for the moment; the rest of the world certainly has.

Lawyers weren't hated in the decades past. Remember *Night Court*? That show was full of lawyers, and everyone loved it. Today, women have bumblefucked their way into 44 percent of first-year law students, and guess what? Now everyone fucking hates lawyers.

Women have an aura of ruination about them. The French probably have a cool word for it, but I don't know French because I'm a man. Perhaps it has something to do with their two half-retarded X chromosomes. If you've ever tried to force two similarly charged magnets together, you know that it doesn't work.

Imagine a woman. What's she doing? Is she marrying someone who gave her gonorrhea? Or is she just still fucking him and keeping a bottle of Suprax under the pillow? Maybe she's convincing her boyfriend not to take an incredible job overseas because she wants to sit around Miami-Dade

County, Florida, with her bitch friends and pursue a master's in art history?

The point is, women lawyers are just women in fancy suits with three-year JS degrees in the school of keeping their yaps shut.

Law school is Chinese water torture for women, but instead of water getting dropped in one spot for three years, women are just made to look like the dumbest imbeciles on earth every time they open their mouths. It's mouth-shutting training, and I recommend that all women go to law school. But for fuck's sake, don't let them practice law.

When your woman lawyer drops your case to get pregnant, you will find yourself in the lurch with a fistful of subpoenas and an assful of foot from your ex-wife's co-council.

Being a lawyer and being a man make a person a unique combination of equity and fairness. That's why men invented the law. Being a lawyer and being a woman makes a person a sexual-harassment nightmare. As if the world needed any more frivolous lawsuits.

2. Soldier

Women have no place in anything where incompetence doesn't equal results. That means women have no place anywhere except attracting a mate and fucking up their birth control. Men are suckers for damsels in distress. We men value honesty in our life partners, and we realize that women who constantly fuck up are merely being honest with us. Fucking up for women is almost a virtue.

But let's not get silly here. This isn't a book about slap-dicking and patting women on the back. Fucking up for women is not a real virtue, because they're not doing it on purpose. No one can fault women for their incompetence. We can only fault them for lying about it.

The Marine Corps is the toughest branch in the military, comprising America's top 1 percent. Now America's bottom 50 percent, women, think someone saved them a seat at the table. Sorry, ladies, the table of honor is reserved.

We men kind of man-fucked ourselves here. With all the technological fucking wonderments we invented, like satellites and wrist communicators, women in the military have automatic compensation for their cartographically-challenged brains and their inability to communicate. It's also our fault for keeping the world so fucking safe for the last fifty years. I can barely remember the name of the last major war, and women can't even remember that constantly talking about blow jobs makes them sound like sluts. How the fuck are they supposed to remember history? More than likely, they've forgotten that the Army is all about fighting in wars and not about getting free money for plastic surgery.

Any female soldier who says she's enlisting for the right reasons is full of shit. Women never do anything for the right reasons. Sure, they drive to places and eventually figure out how to turn on your stereo even though you expressly fuck-ing told them not to touch it, but rest assured, they weren't doing any of it on purpose. Women might get to the end of

the maze without having their hands held, but they don't
know how it happened. It's just random, like a blind chicken
pecking in the dark.

The right reasons for joining the Army are honor and
country and the protection of liberties. G.I. Jane wouldn't
know the right reasons if they waltzed up and offered to help
her carry something heavy, like her gun.

Women treat war like they treat divorces or stolen parking spaces. It's their chance to stick it to the other guy, and
if there's a chance someone is going to get his dick cut off
while no one's looking, then that would be just fantastic.
Can you imagine such a sick mentality at play on the battle-
field? I've seen women pull shit at day care centers that the
Nazis would've denounced.

3. Doctor

Women are killing us.

I mean that figuratively, like when you tell a woman to
change the channel from her stupid show on Lifetime and she
asks you which remote is for the TV for the fuck-hundredth
time. The TV doesn't change the channel, the cable box does.
That kills me figuratively.

But women are also killing us literally, too.

Any med school diversity handout organization will tell
you that young women are breaking down the barriers of the
medical profession. They're actually breaking down not just
the barriers, but the whole medical profession.

Statistics from the University of Cape Town Medical School tell me something I already knew: Women are lazy as fuck. After taking up valuable space in med school, female graduates follow their lackluster educations with lackluster specializations. These female specializations include psychiatry, pediatrics, obstetrics, and the most wasted specialty of them all: motherhood. Women suck up medical degrees like they're inexhaustible, only to throw them right into the trash along with the placenta.

If I can't get a new liver because some lady doctor was on her goldbrick, eighteen-month maternity leave, I will be pretty upset. Not that it would matter to her, of course. Once women have children, that's all they care about. About three days after having a kid, a woman discovers the endless rewards of a career in lazy babysitting.

Being a mother and raising children is the easiest fucking thing in the world. Being a doctor is the opposite. Motherhood is a million times easier than psychiatry and pediatrics and whatever other bullshit specialization women cop out with, and motherhood is especially about a billion times easier than brain surgery and liver transplants and all gory jobs medical men specialize in.

Men grab healing by the balls.

4. Civil Servant

Last Tuesday I spent the evening on my porch with a fine cigar and a glass of that Rare Kentucky Bourbon. I was attempting to light my cigar with an entire book of matches because I had seen someone do that on television and it looked really cool, only to find that matches are more flammable than they look. As I stomped out the book of matches and a small trash-can fire, I found myself thinking: *If I had just caught the house on fire, would I feel safe knowing there's a two percent chance my rescue could be blundered by a lady fireman? Two percent of firemen are ladies.*

Men are better than women at being firemen and policemen and any other job that ends in "men." Men are stronger with our muscles and we're faster with our feet. What more proof do you need? How about a built-in hose? What woman knows how to properly handle a hose? And what lady fireman could carry a burning child from a burning building with the giant chip she's got on her shoulder? Supporting lady policemen and lady firemen kills burning children. As men, it's our responsibility to look after our burning children. Who the fuck else is going to do it?

Thousands of people have suffered in a crisis due to women's lack of strength, speed, and quick, rational thinking. You can blame female firefighters for that. And even more people have been bored to death because someone couldn't tell a funny joke about some lady doing something dumb because there was a woman around. You can thank *all* women for that.

I dropped my wallet down a storm drain one time, and because I couldn't tear the steel grating out of the ground, I lost it. Well, fuck me . . . but imagine if that wallet were a baby, and that steel grate were some kind of problem that required a brain. If I were a lady policeman, that baby would have sailed straight down the drain on a raft of incompetence.

5. Teacher

Children are our future. Half of them are, anyway. And fucking up with children is almost as bad as fucking up ourselves, real-time. I have never learned anything from a female teacher except how to lose control of a classroom. Everything else I've ever learned has been from a man.

There are a handful of questions you can ask any woman to get her to talk about deep, personal things—which is another way of saying mindless, repetitive bullshit that will get you laid. Women are like outboard motors of sex. No matter how long they've been sitting, you just have to give them the right yank in the form of "appearing to give a shit," and they'll be purring in seconds.

One effective yank is the question, "Who was your best schoolteacher?"

All women have a "best" teacher and it's always some other woman. Unless they fucked their favorite teacher; then it's a man. A woman naming a "best" schoolteacher is like the town drunk awarding his imaginary friend a Pulitzer Prize. What the fuck does either of them know about the Pulitzer Prize? That it's good? That's about all women know about teaching. That, and they get three months off in the summer.

Women can't teach anything, which is why they brag about being good nurturers.

You know what nurturing means? It means adding nothing. It means taking a situation and encouraging whatever is going on to continue. Nurturing means being the fucking middle manager of life, sitting on your doughy ass and putting a rubber stamp on things that you really had nothing to do with. Nurturing means collecting thank-yous.

All teachers who charge their students money are male. Tutors, trade teachers, university professors—they're all men. That proves men are better than women at teaching. Strippers are better than regular women at getting naked for the same reason.

You can't expect a fifth grader to waltz into an advanced physics course and pick up a lecture in mid-stride. That's exactly how it is with women opening their mouths for the purpose of imparting knowledge. Women have looked at every advancement of our species—fire, money, clothing, justice, planes, trains, and automobiles—with the attitude of "Fuck it, I'll learn about it later." What they really meant was "Fuck it, I'll fuck for it later."

You don't have to teach that, because all women figure it out at fifteen and then retire their brains.

6. Dentist

For fun, let's say you are afraid of the dentist. Well, that just makes you one smart motherfucker. Take a virtual walk through the office of your local dental practitioner. See the receptionists? Wow, they're women. The hygienists? Women. Jesus, these days women can even get dental degrees and open up shop themselves—just as long as some man puts his name on the door. No one wants to see Dr. Barbie Barbarella.

Per capita, there's a higher percentage of women in the dental industry than there is in yoga, Singles for Cons mailing lists, and Chocaholics Anonymous combined. With an unmanned herd like that running the show, is it any surprise dentists are fucked and everyone is scared shitless of them? Like lawyers, women are the reason everyone hates dentists. Ten seconds of getting my gums cleaned by a lady dentist, and I was ready to knock someone the fuck out—either her or myself, whichever was less illegal. If going to the dentist were a game of Clue, the answer would be: Dick Masterson, in the bedroom, with the Vicodin.

Gum disease is no laughing matter, and thanks to women and their incompetence and lust for inflicting pain, no one wants to get their teeth checked. Women are also the reason they won't put porn on during a root canal. I guess at the dentist's office, the customer *isn't* always right.

7. Valet

Have you ever heard someone say the following after a horrible car accident?

"At least you're okay. It could have been much worse. You could have been hurt!"

Well, that someone was a woman. There's nothing worse than having a destroyed car and not having a single scratch on yourself. It feels cowardly. Cars are not things to be used and then tossed out like garbage or last week's bar skank. A car is a manly thing designed with precision and built for service. It deserves respect. If my car is fucked up, I want to at least have a broken arm or a broken ass. I'm a man. A woman should never, ever, ever be a valet. Being a valet is the deadliest job a woman can have. Here's why:

The modern world is built on the service industry. I don't know what the third world is built on; I guess sewage. In the modern world, the service industry empties our garbage; it restocks our shelves; it gets food from the farm to the processing factory and then straight into our children's mouths where it belongs. The service industry is an army of men that finds what you want and gets it to you as fast as fucking possible.

Things like your car.

Women shouldn't be doctors or pilots, but if they are, a mere handful of lives are endangered—ten thousand, tops. What happens when women start being valets? Then they'd want to become trash collectors and truck drivers. Then what?

A civilization-ending catastrofuck, that's what. Trash cans all over the face of the earth spill into the streets as garbage-women do their hair. Huge swaths of forest overtake cities as lumberjacks adjust their pantyhose. Schoolchildren go without the precious paper they need for learning. And, perhaps worst of all, your brand-new car gets the shit dinged out of it.

If women were valets, plumbers, and air-conditioning repairmen, the whole fucking world would fall apart. And before it did, it would get dinged.

Here's why this dystopian future will never happen. Let me present a hypothetical question asked of the first potential female valet by her potential boss.

Boss: "Can you drive a stick shift?"

No woman can drive a stick shift. If you disagree, go look up the word "drive" in a dictionary and then kiss my ass. Here's something else women don't know, and I swear to God this is true and happened to me: Women don't know that the ticket stub the valet gives you is the secret to getting your car back. Apparently it's a big fucking mystery to women how the valet always brings back the correct car.

"Valets must have really good memories," a woman I was about to fuck once said to me.

"They sure do," I said. Men have good memories too—we remember to keep the world spinning.

COOKING UP TROUBLE

To be a great chef it takes dedication, a knowledge of various spices, and some amount of sensitivity. Men have so much dedication and sensitivity that it's coming out our asses. Women have none of those things. Knowing that cinnamon tastes good on frappucinos, or whatever candy-ass coffee that costs $3.95 (not that she's paying), is not a knowledge of spices.

The kind of chefs women make are the Martha Stewarts of the world: convicts slapping glitter on pinecones.

When a man is a chef, he makes plans and then he executes them, man-style. Man-style means as directly as a fucking comet. That's why everything a man makes tastes exactly like it's supposed to. When a woman is a chef, she behaves as all women behave all the time: traipsing around like a drunken marionette with her head in Cabo San Lucas and without a thought in the world for consequences. Women are terrible chefs because they ricochet off their own dramas like a pinball, never knowing what in the fuck is going on and never having half a shit to give. They're like lopsided bowling balls on a golf course.

Note also that the title "chef" cannot be bastardized into the feminine form. For example, women can be policewomen, but a woman can't be a cheftress or a chefwoman. This can also be said for the title of judge.

WOMEN NURSES ARE GROSS

In the fifties, women kept their mouths shut. That's probably why there was so much less homosexuality in the fifties.

Without all that gabbing, the fifties woman was able to focus on doing four jobs half-competently instead of doing many jobs worthlessly. These jobs were cooking, cleaning, drink-freshening, and nursing.

Today's modern woman is different than her fifties counterpart. She's fatter, first of all. Also, she won't shut up, she can't cook, she's a complete mess, and worst of all, she's a shitty nurse.

Men have a little thing called class that gets us through the day. For example, men who are in the army or who are pilots wear snappy uniforms. That's classy. We men accept responsibility for our actions and our appearance, and we know we will be judged on both.

Women don't accept responsibility for how they look or act. Go on a prostitute scavenger hunt down Main Street of Anytown, Earth, to prove that for yourself. You're going to guess wrong ninety-nine out of ninety-nine times.

What about male doctors? You better believe they conduct themselves with class—shitloads of class. Women nurses, however, conduct themselves like high school cheerleaders. They're gabby as shit, and they have heads full of boys and sawdust.

I was shopping for a new pair of shoelaces the other day. I like to put my shoes on the same way I start the day: like I'm revving up a fucking chainsaw. That's why I've gone through four sets of shoelaces for this particular pair of shoes. While running this errand, I spotted a herd of nurses walking out of the mall.

Do you know how I knew they were nurses? It wasn't because they looked like they enjoyed hanging a little bit of power over the heads of people with broken arms and kids with whooping cough. I knew they were nurses because they were still wearing their fucking nurse scrubs.

Women nurses wear their blood-smocks to the supermarket.

There is no class in that. If *Sesame Street* had a Muppet who taught kids about venereal disease, women nurses would be less classy than that Muppet.

Could there be anything more crass, insensitive, and careless than a nurse wearing her used hospital rags to a public place? What about those of us who have recently experienced traumatic personal loss? That kind of thing happens in a hospital, and I'll be damned if I'm supposed to sit there and choke on a churro about it while watching a bunch of nurses sitting around talking about *Grey's Anatomy*. Also, someone might have pissed on those scrubs. Now they're just sitting around in the food court wafting piss all over the place? Gross.

As usual, women wear everything they do like a sash of merit badges at all times, even when it's not a big deal. Women can't be subtle about anything. A woman aches all day to clumsily blurt out something stupid about herself during a conversation—especially if she's just met you. Then it'll be something extra stupid like her thoughts on God. Who the fuck are they kidding? If women were garbagemen, they'd drag bags of shit into Starbucks with them.

THERE GOES THE JUDGE

Did you know that during the last century as many as two women sat on the Supreme Court of the United States?

Now, I can appreciate a good practical joke, and everyone knows Ronald Reagan was a cut-up, but *two*?

If there's anything women don't understand and can't appreciate, it's a gesture of charity done twice. Women are like Las Vegas. You can pull off some crazy shit in a casino once, but the next time you step in the door, you're going to get punched in your nards. That's why married women don't get flowers. If women were appreciative the first time they got them, then their apartments would look like a florist's shop.

If you are unfamiliar with the United States legal system, the Supreme Court is a body of like twelve or nine people who draw the line between right and wrong. They say you can do this, you can't do that, and if you do too much of that, we'll fuck you up. If courts were ranked in terms of road construction contract difficulties, the Supreme Court would be a collapsed freeway on top of a volcano. Does that sound like somewhere you'd want a woman calling the shots? When you're dangling over a volcano with a rivet gun in your hand and a billion tons of molten lava under your ass?

Sure, women are great at saying what you can't do. They're pessimists and think everything every man does is wrong. There's no judgment involved there. Women choose one and only one ideology their whole lives. They make up their minds about everything when they're thirteen years old, and then they cling to that mantra like a broken buoy. Huge waves of information and learning crash on the heads of women, but the buoy keeps them from succumbing to those waves.

A judge shouldn't be afraid to mix it up when he thinks getting the job done requires ruffling a few feathers in the establishment. A judge takes a look at the facts and says, "Look, you bastard, is this getting anybody laid?"

That's called jurisprudence.

THEY CAN NEVER TAKE OUR PIMPDOM

If prostitution was the first profession, then pimping was the second.

Ask any prostitute and she'll tell you that pimps are essential to the trade. Without a pimp, prostitutes run risks like forgetting to take their birth control and something having to do with stalkers. It's also hard out there for a pimp; no prostitute has ever won an Oscar for best soundtrack.

Men invented pimping to clean up the mess women made with their first career choice: whoring it up like the earth was the biggest *Girls Gone Wild* set in the universe.

The only successful woman pimp ever, Heidi Fleiss, was so inept she not only went to prison, but she nearly sullied the reputation of one of the greatest thespians of the twentieth century: Charlie Sheen. How's that for being discreet? Discretion is the second rule of pimping. That's why pimps always dress so stylishly. No one bothers looking at the clientèle when they can look at a cane with a golden monkey head on it.

And when I say Heidi Fleiss was "successful," I mean

that in the only way women can be "successful"—by sleeping her way to the top and dodging the tornado of her own ineptitude for as long as womanly possible. Ultimately, success for a woman comes down to getting the new high score for Most Years Without Fucking Up. I think the record is like two. Eleanor Roosevelt probably holds it. I don't really know, and I probably don't give a shit.

Pimping requires business sense, charisma, compassion, and debonairness. A woman has never had any of those.

Let's look at the facts:

Pimps cannot take maternity leave.
Pimps cannot afford to dress inappropriately for work.
Pimps cannot start crying while business is going on around them.

Pimping has been around ever since the first woman saw the first man building a shelter, making dinner, and inventing vegetables, and thought to herself, "I can't do any of that shit. Guess I better learn how to fuck."

And she never did.

PRESTO, CHANGE-O! WOMEN ARE SHITTY MAGICIANS

There has never been a good woman magician.

Women are important to magic, but it's in the same way

that women are important to office work: short skirts.

Men are better than women at being showmen, but that doesn't explain why there has never been a good woman magician. Why can't Oprah pop a trick or two out of her fat ass every once in a while? How about Ellen? Turning Anne Heche straight again was a pretty good trick; why couldn't she be a good magician?

Women make shitty magicians because they believe in magic. They believe in it with every ounce of their being.

Take sending a quarter through a table; women believe that actually happened. They're terrified by it too. If a guy can force you to pick a two of spades twice in a row, where the fuck does this power stop?

Luckily, I'm a man, and men don't buy bullshit on any level. That's for women. Women buy bullshit like no one's making any more of it—for instance, that people who say "I love you" mean it no matter what, or that turning an orange into some guy's retirement watch which just a few minutes ago was broken in a velour bag is some kind of fucking miracle.

Nope. It's bullshit.

Men are the purveyors of bullshit, not consumers of it, and it's that fucking simple. We sell boatloads of bullshit like magic and telling little kids they're doing a good job when any idiot can see they suck at everything. We sell it, but we don't buy it. We don't walk around with our fairy-tale diaries in hand, looking to add another fuckup we didn't see coming a mile away.

PILOT ERROR

Everyone has heard stories of people who decide at the very last moment not to take a flight, and then the plane crashes and everyone dies spectacularly. Everyone dies except the person who didn't get on the plane.

Well, that very thing happened to me recently. I was about to board a plane to London and there was a woman in a snappy blue uniform next to me. I asked her why she was wearing that outfit.

"I'm the pilot."

I took the next flight.

I don't know if that plane crashed, and I don't give a fuck. I wouldn't feel stupid for not jumping off a freeway overpass just because a mattress truck happened to drive under it at the exact moment I would have landed. Jumping off a freeway overpass is always a stupid thing to do. And so is flying in a winged donkey cart if a woman is *womanning* the throttle. Just because she luckily made it for the twelfth time in a row doesn't mean it's now a good idea.

Piloting requires a bunch of shit women can't do. Women can't read dials or maps, they don't understand how wings work if it doesn't involve their underpants, and they sure as shit can't work a joystick. (That's a bit of subtle penis humor.)

But the biggest reason there are no women pilots is that women are afraid of greatness.

There's an old and dumb saying that goes, "Behind every great man, there is a woman." That's true, but that woman is behind the man cowering in fear from the thunderous applause and adoration that a great man receives, like how a dog cowers behind the couch when the vacuum cleaner is on.

Women's fear of success is why they've got such a hard-on for teamwork; that's why no one gives a shit each year when a new woman is inducted into the Women Who Have Made a Difference Hall of Fame. Those women haven't made any difference. What the fuck has any woman ever done, ever, let alone each year?

Yes, it would be criminally negligent to give a woman the throttle of an aircraft. But the real reason woman pilots don't exist is because no woman ever looked up into the great blue sky and said, "I wish I was up there. I wish I *was something.*"

Women are the sum of their impulses, unreliable in the present and intangible to history. If you're thinking about flying with a lady pilot, just remember these two words: Amelia Earhart. You'll know what to do.

WOMEN MAKE SHITTY MUSICIANS

Every once in a while, I hear college girls asking each other the following:

"If women and men are supposed to be equal, then why do we make such shitty musicians?"

I'm joking. I've never heard women at any level of babysitting ask each other such an honest question. I do disagree with the question though. And as a man, I can disagree with eye rolls, questions, and other nonstatements, despite the fact that women think keeping their mouths shut gives them *carte blanche* for atrocious behavior.

Women make shitty musicians the same way McDonald's makes shitty pizza. Which is to say, what the fuck are you talking about?

Think of the greatest composers in history. That's easy. You've got your Mozart and your Beethoven, you've got your Bach, but what about the not-so-greats? You could probably do some digging on the Internet—and if you were a woman you could convince a man to do some digging on the Internet and then talk about the results like you fucking knew all of them already, because as a woman you pull that manner of shit all the time. What you'd find in the annals of music is a sausage party so jam-packed with men it belongs about a block from the airport. Music and women are natural enemies, just like women and beer. Women hate people having a good time, and they're outrageous control freaks. Women practice too goddamn much to be any good at music. Practice is a silly and womanly thing. It's just prancing around the sidelines while the real job gets done on the field.

Here's a good question: If women and men are equal—which they're fucking not—then why hasn't there ever been a female Mozart? Why hasn't some little girl ever hopped off her daddy's lap and composed a masterpiece for the ages?

THESPIANISM AND FEMINISM

I've got a brilliant plan to make a Hollywood disaster film. I don't mean a disaster film like with radioactive tornadoes, I mean a disaster film as in a massive box office failure. A career-ending accounting disaster. A film in which no dollars are recouped and no market is impacted. A failure so bad, cash actually pours out of the bank like tears.

Are you ready for it? Here's the idea: Have a woman star in the leading role.

Just like the first time they let a woman on the space shuttle, any movie that allows a woman to helm the leading role will be a huge fucking catastrophe.

Here's a list of the top-grossing movies of all time:

1. *Titanic*—male lead
2. *Star Wars*—male lead
3. *Shrek 2*—male ogre lead
4. *E.T.*—male alien lead

The list goes on, so I'll stop there, because this book is not about going on and on. It's about getting to the point. That's manly.

Nowhere in the top 100 highest grossing films of all time is there a single female lead character. The only movie where a woman might even be important at all is *What Women Want* starring Mel Gibson, and I say "might be" because I haven't seen that movie and nothing on earth could make me. *Snow White* was about dwarves, *My Fat Fuck Wedding* was about two hours too long, and if you think *Gone with the Wind* had anything to do with that uppity whore Scarlet, then frankly my dear, I don't give a damn.

Acting requires a familiarity with all kinds of emotions, but the only emotions women know are greed and jealousy. Women can't act, they can't sing, and they're not funny. They have as much place in the public forum as a mule has in a beauty pageant, yet still they stumble in with their sashes clamped between their teeth braying for time in the spotlight. Women will do anything for attention: good attention, bad attention, the worst kind of attention; it doesn't matter. Women are so addicted to attention that if prostitution were legal, it would also be free. But why don't women give a shit about movies based on the lives of women? Not even they give a shit, because a main character who latches on to everything like a leech, ruins all she touches like a reverse Midas, and has absolutely no redeeming qualities, makes for a shitty story. Just describing a female character ruined this paragraph. Now imagine two and a half hours of it.

Now *that's* a disaster film.

A WOMAN PRESIDENT? MORE LIKE, NO FUCKING WAY

I hate to be political as much as the next man—which means that I love it more than I love breathing air or using my eyeballs for seeing.

Men would rather talk about politics than do anything else. Men would rather talk about politics than have sex. That's how incredible we are. We are always looking out for the greater good instead of selfishly and womanly thinking about ourselves. Also, you don't have to clean anything up after a political discussion.

Politics is in the blood of men as much as getting animals drunk and being forever vigilant for the greatest and fastest shortcut of all time. Politics is a quest. But for what? Bam, that's what. That's called Man Zen, and if you were a woman, that would have blown your mind. As a man, however, the notion fits your mind like a sixty dollar pair of underpants.

Let us picture a mythical land that would embody only the manliest of natures. I'm talking about Valhalla, but Germany works too. Picnic benches of oak as thick as cinder blocks stretch as far as the eye can see. You can smash beer steins the weight of airplane windshields together with drunken abandon for the absolute fuck of it. This is the kind of place where having the wrong opinion will get you punched in the mouth. Manly.

In such a place, no one cares how anyone's day was or how their parents are to blame for every single fuckup in their lives—even the fuckups their parents specifically told them not to do. It's all politics, all the time. And you can no sooner squelch the desire for politics in men than you can shove a Dumpster into the middle of the street with your bare hands. They're, like, a hundred times heavier than they look.

A woman will never ever in a million years be president of the United States or of anywhere. You can tout and tally all the polls and surveys you want, but the only poll you need to listen to is the one that makes you a man—and that is your penis.

What man has time to jerk around answering stupid surveys about voting for the president anyway? Men are too busy actually being the president. Women probably think they're actually voting when they participate in those stupid polls. Observe as I blow the lid off the hype and media bullshit.

No woman will ever be president because:

1. No woman is a man.
2. See rule 1.

Done.

Women understand politics as much as a screwdriver understands crossing a busy street. Sure, you can carry a screwdriver to the store and buy it a cookie, but in the end it has no goddamn idea what's going on. If a woman is ever elected president, I will eat this book.

CHAPTER 2

The Skills to Pay No Bills

I was going to call this book Dick Masterson's Guide to Life, but then I realized that would be a very short book.

Dick Masteron's Guide to Life
1. Shut up.
2. Get the job done.

That's why women are such failures. Step 1, shutting up, is an impossible hurdle for their overloaded female brains. Even if their gray matter wasn't clogged with puppies and posting hunks on their MySpace pages, women still couldn't shut the fuck up. They could quit their jobs and take pep pills until the Apocalypse, but they still wouldn't have enough time to talk about golden retrievers.

Step 2, getting the job done, requires getting the job, and getting the job requires making a fucking resumé, which no woman in the world can do.

If women have to present themselves in a way that doesn't involve straps, no-straps, or double-sided tape, they completely fuck it up. Men are like chameleons when it comes to presentation. You could take James Bond and drop him off on a farm in the middle of Iowa, and if you turned your back for even a second, he would blend in like the toothpaste in the holes in the walls of my first apartment.

Resumés do not suit the frail and vindictive monster that is the female ego. Why should a woman make a resumé? Isn't everything you need to know about hiring her written all over her soul?

No woman has ever made her own resumé. They've all had a man do it for them. Go find a woman and ask her. I fucking guarantee that you will get the following answer:

Well, my boyfriend/father made my first resumé, but it was just my first!

Resumés aren't fashion items or countries from which female celebrities steal babies. They don't change radically from year to year. Resumés are more like the list of imaginary grievances married women carry around in their heads at all times. They get made once very early on, and they just get new shit tacked on each year:

1995—Doesn't like that I've blossomed into a full-figured woman.

1997—Venerated the book I bought on psychic healing.

1997—Made fun of me for not knowing what "venerated" meant.

2002—Didn't pick up on my hints about wanting more jewelry.

No matter how good at bullshitting you are, you can't phrase "got paid for doing fucking nothing" in a way that makes employers trip all over themselves with stock options. Maybe there's a gender pay gap because every woman's resumé looks like this:

> *Her Name*
> *Seeking: A job.*
> *Objective: Keep job with minimum effort.*
> *Skills: Can't make a simple fucking resumé.*

I would say that's the stupidest resumé I've ever seen, but as soon as I wrote it, I realized women could fuck it up even worse. Like with glitter stickers or by printing it on stationery covered in Hello Kitty.

I can hear the wage gap growing like cracks in the mantle crust.

THE TOOLS OF THE TRADE

The only tool men need to get any job done is one we already have. It's a tool we've had since birth, and it's also the source of our manliest drives. It's a tool that serves many purposes and is one that women don't have and they crave it constantly. This tool is responsible for the greatest achievements known to the species. It transcends generations and will have an impact on philosophy, music, and literature for all time. It's also enormously big.

This great tool is a man's brain. I bet you thought I was talking about The Penis.

Well, actually, I was.

NATURE'S FILIBUSTER

Arguing with a woman is like walking through a fun house of mirrors.

It's amusing for a while, and it's cheap. You get to see yourself in new and interesting ways and maybe do some reflection and emotional maturing. Men love maturing. Fuck, some days I mature more during my morning shit than any woman has ever done in her whole life. Looking at mirrors means talking to the man in the mirror, maybe asking him to change his ways.

But then it gets really fucking irritating and disorienting, because almost none of it makes any sense, and you have to keep backtracking to make progress that you thought you made ten minutes ago. You probably also have to go to the bathroom, but fuck you—there's no way out.

Women define losing an argument as not having the last word.

It's a stupid and backward mindset, because in the end nobody learns anything about anything, but that's how women do it. Think you're getting somewhere with a woman in a debate about politics or business? Guess again. You've just spoken. That means she's about to lose. Strap on your gloves, buddy, because you're in for another round. And if you think I mean boxing gloves, you've just made a big mistake. Arguing with a woman isn't verbal pugilism, it's wading through a torrent of verbal shit. Put on your shit-shoveling gloves.

A man's idea of argumentation is threefold:

1. Identify the issue.
2. Gather research and information regarding the (same) issue.
3. Reach a resolution.

Women are nature's filibuster. They argue like this:

1. Waste as much time as possible.
2. Get nowhere.

Women value time like a garbage disposal values fine cuisine. It's just something else to grind up and flush away. How can they even understand the concept of time wasted when they have nothing to do with it anyway?

WOMEN CAN'T SPELL FOR SHIT

Did you know that women are atrocious spellers? To prove this, I've compiled a short list of words women have historically suffered complete and disastrous failure when attempting to spell.

Dick's List of Words Women Can't Spell
Chevrolet
bullion
kernels
sandwich
duct tape
beans
trophy

If you want to put this to a test—and have quite a ripping laugh at the absurd letters women throw out in desperation—prepare for a struggle. While men face adversity like we're new basketball coaches at run-down inner-city high schools, women quit things after a few seconds.

When you ask a woman to do anything she sucks at—driving, having sex in the light, any kind of thinking that doesn't involve how much she hates her best friends—that woman will immediately delegate the task to the nearest man. This includes spelling. And it also includes asking a woman if North and South Dakota are two parts of one big state or two entirely different states. Women don't even know that.

Since it is part of our man-nature to be of assistance and to be constructive and positive at all times, because we know so goddamn much about so many things, men are always helpful. When men see a damsel in distress, we jump in and punch the fuck out of something. Sometimes it's a mugger or a dragon, but sometimes it's some unspelled words.

I asked a group of ten women to spell the word "foundation." I chose "foundation" because I heard on an episode of *CSI* that it had something to do with makeup. My hypothesis was that this word-familiarity would give women the handicap they desperately need in everything they do.

My results not only proved conclusively that women cannot spell, but that women will refuse to do any task beyond their abilities and that they will also call me a jerk.

To a woman, the alphabet and its inner workings are like the mysteries of a jack-in-the-box to a child.

Women can't spell "failure." They can live it, but they can't spell it.

WOMEN SUCK AT COMPUTERS

Computers are all over the place: banks, science labs, the workplace. In other words, computers are everywhere women are not.

To women, computers are like a man being thrilled as hell when his best buddy gets dumped and then has to rely on his friends for emotional support. That doesn't make any sense to us. Computers are that way for women.

Women don't understand computers because they don't understand cause and effect; one thing causes the other. It's childlike in its simplicity, I know, but it's way too complicated for women. That's why women are always just about to hopelessly fuck up their lives by doing the exact same thing they've fucked up before, but this time expecting it to magically work. That's why women are so fat. They think they're eventually going to eat a magic carb that turns them into Heidi Klum.

I saw this misunderstanding of cause and effect just yesterday while waiting in line for an ATM. For some absurd reason, a woman had been given an ATM card, which she promptly lost in the ATM. The woman began frantically pressing buttons like an enraged stenographer, expecting at any moment something profoundly contrary to what had been happening so far.

Guess what? It didn't happen.

Every time a man drops a rock, he knows it's going to fall. Women think if they do it enough times, it will turn into a Snickers bar.

GIVE A MOOSE A MUFFIN, WOMEN ARE INCONSIDERATE

Consideration and politeness are the reasons why men don't ask for directions.

Giving directions is a huge pain in the ass. As inconvenience goes, it ranks right up there under "helping a friend move" and "ordering porno in secret." Not only do you have to think of a bunch of fucking directions, but you also have to try and remember what you were thinking about for later when you're done walking some rude jackass down the street in your mind. Women don't know how much of a pain in the ass giving directions is, because no one on earth has ever asked a woman how to get anywhere. What would be the point of that? It would be like punching a valet in the stomach as you handed over your keys. Hope you like shit in your backseat.

A woman asking another woman for directions would be a hilarious late-night talk show bit, actually. One of those bits where everyone laughs at how outlandish and absurd someone can be when they have no fucking idea what they're talking about.

Men also don't like inconveniencing other men by asking them to move all their shit from one apartment to another. Women have no idea how inconvenient it is to move all of someone's shit, because their idea of moving is to wear a baseball cap for a day.

When a woman thinks she's being considerate or nice, what she really does is something that she wants to do anyway and then prepares a torrent of fury in case she's not honored like a war hero for doing it.

CINDER BLOCKS ARE TO COMFORTABLE AS WOMEN ARE TO CLEVER

Do you know why women don't think the Three Stooges are funny? Because women aren't funny. The Three Stooges are as hilarious as it gets.

To a woman, "funny" isn't a special thing like it is to a man. It's not a way to relax or blow off steam. What steam do women have to blow off? They don't have jobs, and if they do, they don't have any responsibilities at their jobs, so what the fuck?

To a woman, being "funny" means saying something obvious and then laughing like a mule. Usually the things women say to make themselves laugh don't even have jokes in them. They're just crass, untrue things. Female comedy is like tofu comedy. It looks like comedy, but it's actually some kind of bean curd—or something. I don't know what tofu is. I'm a man.

Men, on the other hand, are magic comedy-machines able to pull off incredible feats of funny whenever it's required. Watch and I'll prove this now by thinking of something funny right off the top of my head. I don't even have to try. I'm already thinking of it preemptively. In fact, I bet all of us men are thinking of something fresh and hilarious, I just want to make the point. Okay, here comes something funny.

Picture a chicken sitting in a nest on a grass field. It's a pretty close-up shot. Then the chicken gets up and checks some eggs it's sitting on. They're doing just fine. Then a man wearing full football gear comes running in from the side and punts the chicken through some goalposts.

That is hilarious. And any man is able to produce something equally or more funny on demand.

Part of the reason women are not funny is that they are

not fun. To a woman, having fun and being happy is the man-equivalent of getting kicked in the groin—which is also hilarious. Women also are not funny because they can't listen for shit. You can't improve your material when you can't hear everyone not laughing. Women will also henpeck the shit out of each other for trying to make a joke. I call that the Female Albatross of Failure.

When men aren't keeping the world spinning, all we do is sit around and practice being hilarious. Women sit around giving each other backhanded compliments.

CURSE WORDS MAKE SUGARPLUM FAIRIES CRY

I can't even count the number of times I've been chastised by some undersexed schoolmarm who should have been minding her own fucking business for tossing a few bawdy words into a conversation. What the fuck?

As a man I use swear words, or "sentence enhancers," with extreme discretion and in proper taste at all times. I'm like a dancing word chef with a bottomless tub of Bacon Bits, ready to dish them out like a ninja all over your meal and your face. Fuck!

That's not enough for women, though, because it's perfectly reasonable and it's not shiny and expensive. Women have no interest in that kind of thing.

Women claim swearing is uncouth or inappropriate. That's the stupidest thing I have ever heard in all the history of stupid shit that I have heard. Women are so inappropriate it makes me sick. Just go and look at a woman half your age. She looks like a complete whore. Now think about this: A man twice your age who is reading this book is thinking the same thing about the woman you're currently with. How's that for a mind blow?

Man Zen.

Women hate swearing, because they think curse words are magical and cursed.

Women believe in fairies and Easter bunnies and princesses in faraway castles. They're raised on bullshit like calves on bonemeal, and it's so ingrained in their psyches that the process of immersing themselves in wild delusion and fantastic drama governs every waking moment of their lives.

The truth is, fellows and gentlemen, that swearing puts asses in the seats. Swearing gives something with no credibility a shitload of credibility. Swearing is how you make a good point a great fucking point.

Men like to make things better with our man-tools, be they literal man-tools, like a wrench or an anvil, or figurative man-tools, like swearing or thinking or a round of fisticuffs. Points, seats, and quality of life are all the same in a man's world. They're all things to improve.

Women, on the other hand, prefer to invent crazy reasons not to use the tools God gave them: swear words, their brains, their vaginas.

Repeal the 19th Amendment before swearing is made illegal.

DRESS FOR FAILURE DOESN'T RHYME

Have you ever heard a woman talk about a man wearing a suit? Good Lord, it's disgusting. They drool like starved jackals.

If women are so obsessed with how men dress, why do all women dress like complete shit?

Walk down any street and see how many men have dressed poorly for the work week. You might see a few teenagers who haven't quite gotten it figured out yet, but otherwise you'll see nothing but impeccable class. You'll see men wearing business suits and smart-looking blazers, both of which are more appropriate for the workplace than a miniskirt and a book with a shirtless dude on the cover.

Even fat dudes will wear fat-fuck Hawaiian shirts and other ingenious pieces of flair, thereby keeping it classy at all times. Fat women just wear out their thesauruses: zaftig, sensual, curvy, comfortable, big-boned, realistic, heavy, big, full-figured, voluptuous, thick, not shallow, oversize, plus-size, buxom, Latin, great personality, real, educated, intelligent, burlesque, Rubenesque, womanesque, juicy, cuddly, BBW, classic, curvaceous, sexy, sassy, average, plump, large-framed, motherly, proportional, pinup style, womanly, pregnant, Amazonian, Victorian, bootylicious. The only thing fat women leave out is any reason to talk to them.

No woman has ever disguised anything about her appearance. Disguise is the first rule of dressing classy like a man. If you've got a gut or a fat ass, draw some attention up to your shoulders or to your money. The first rule of dressing like a woman is to embroider JUICY on whatever body part makes people want to throw up.

Women think everything they wear is great and brilliant, no matter how disgusting it is. They also think the best way to prove this is to shove it in everyone's faces.

The easiest and fastest way to get attention is by making a complete catastrophe of yourself.

CLEANLINESS IS NEXT TO MANLINESS

Think of a woman. If you're anything like me, by which I mean you have a penis, you either thought of Scarlett Johansson or a shrill harpy whirring around the house with a duster and a vacuum cleaner screaming her fucking head off.

For your sake, I hope it was the first one.

When it comes to cleaning, women are possessed by religious fanaticism. One bill in sight or crooked remote control makes her fear an eternity in the Trash Yard of Damnation. Or maybe hell for a woman is forcing her to look in a mirror naked for the rest of time. What a stupid notion of hell that would be for men. Sometimes I'm late to work because I was looking at myself naked for like ten minutes. That's manly.

When women clean, they're a tornado of nerves spinning wildly out of control and flinging the debris of everyday life into neat little piles as though it somehow means anything. That's what women call cleaning: shoving all your shit into drawers like a five-year-old with a learning disability on a reverse scavenger hunt.

Women clean compulsively because their lives are exactly the opposite: a mess. Women think straightening up a book on algebra is the same as inventing it.

Men clean in many stages. That's why we're so good at it. Cleaning is like a fine wine. You can't rush it and if you do, you're surely going to fuck it up. To rush is to not be thorough, and to not be thorough is to not be manly. Cleaning can sometimes take several days or weeks. Rome wasn't built in a day, after all. And when it was done, no one had to clean it up.

Women can take several days getting over a headache, and they can take several days getting back on a diet after downing a German chocolate cake in front of the television, but they can't take several days to clean.

Bills

Since women don't pay any bills, they don't know how bills work. If a bill gets put into some random drawer near the kitchen sink and doesn't get paid because bill-paying time doesn't involve treasure maps and interrogations, then women don't understand the consequences. A woman trying to understand bills is like a child grappling with probate law.

When a check is written, put in an envelope, affixed with a stamp, and then set on the edge of the counter only to disappear, that isn't the bill fairy whisking the money away and dropping it magically in the gas company's mailbox. It's a woman thinking she's cleaning up while actually throwing a handful of tacks onto the road that is your life.

The Fucking Remote Control

The remote control can never be cleaned up. It can't be put away, and it can't be clutter, because the remote control is in a constant state of use. Putting the remote in a stupid little basket or box under the coffee table is the equivalent of putting a piano in front of the bathroom door. It may look fancy as fuck, but there's a piano in front of the goddamn bathroom and no way to take a piss.

STUPID QUESTIONS

"There's no such thing as a stupid question," was coined by a woman while she was addressing other women. But without a man around to judge it, is there such a thing as a stupid question? The answer is yes, it is still stupid.

Man Zen.

Here are some questions I have heard women shoot out of their mouths:

"Will it work if I press the wrong button?"

"Are Glade PlugIns electric?"

"How am I supposed to know what 'check engine' means?"

Check engine means the same thing everything else means. It means go find a man as quickly as possible and then soak your feet for an hour while the problem magically fixes itself. If there's a problem of any kind, women should stand perfectly still like they're in one of those rooms with mousetraps and Ping-Pong balls all over the place. One move and the whole shit goes haywire.

THERE IS NO PRINCESS OF LIES

If a man can't explain a cash withdrawal of 300 dollars at 2 a.m. from some ATM in a place his wife or girlfriend has never heard of, who's to say he wasn't just about to purchase something lovely and expensive for that very same woman? The key to giving good gifts is the surprise. Women are so goddamn depraved, they can't think about anything other than booze and whores.

Women lie like a broken 3-D Magic Eye poster. They just chuck out more complicated shit than you can focus your eyeballs at, and the longer you stand there and stare, the less you understand. They sputter and spew a never-ending torrent of shit at you as fast as they can. It's so much information, Encyclopedia Brown's retarded cousin could figure out it was a lie in about two seconds. The crap women come up with doesn't even count as lies. They're just giant run-on sentences sprinkled with the odds you'll probably stop giving a shit halfway through.

Women are impossible to listen to anyway, and you have better things to do with your time. If you can pay attention to a woman for more than two sentences, good for you. You'll figure out she's lying, but you should have known that anyway when sound started coming out of her.

"Lemme get this straight," you might say. "You couldn't hear your cell phone because you were at a club. And then afterward, your friend called you from home because she needed a ride to her mother's house at 10:30, and you could hear the phone then because you were outside smoking at the time, but you couldn't go get her because you left your purse in her car in the first place. And that's why you were late. I only have one question. Without your purse, where the fuck did you get the cigarettes?"

From the dude she's fucking, of course.

WOMEN ARE THE CRAPPIEST VAULT IN THE WORLD

There's an old saying that goes, "Three men can keep a secret so long as two of them are dead." Well, there's a Dick Masterson saying that goes like this: "Two women can keep a secret if both of them are dead." Men have something called integrity. It's what allows that one man to keep a secret. We keep our fucking mouths shut about everything. Men are great.

Take me, your old pal Dick Masterson. I know hundreds of terrible secrets that I've never told anyone. One time I dated a girl named Tracy who liked to bark like a dog during sex.

Disturbing, yes—but it's also humiliating, true, and something I would never divulge.

Men are better than women at keeping secrets, because the only time men betray someone's trust or good faith is when we need to do things like organize an intervention or have a laugh over a pint. Both are noble and benevolent things where everybody wins. Women only tell sec'rets to harvest themselves some sweet pity.

Women will take every secret you tell them and store it away in a bank vault like a doomsday device. As soon as they feel slighted, *BOOM*! It's Showtime at the Apollo with your most embarrassing shit. She and all her friends will come back from the next bar-philandering girls' night out thinking you're some kind of perverted workaholic and incidentally also wanting to fuck the shit out of you. That's how women operate: with no cylinders firing.

Men hold secrets, their opinions, and their feelings in their heads where they belong. Opinions aren't like assholes, they're like testicles. Only men have them and no one should hear them.

DONDE ESTÁ EL COMMON FUCKING COURTESY?

Men invented languages once our thought processes evolved beyond the scope of grunts and pointing. That never happened for women. Anything a woman ever thinks about or wants to say can be expressed in squealing and donkey *hee-haws*. If you need proof of that, just listen to a woman when you're driving a perfectly acceptable distance behind the car in front of you. When it comes to foreign languages, women are a complete joke. A woman who knows a foreign language is like a woman at a bachelorette party: so rude and crass and obsessed with cocks that it makes you sick.

How many of you men have ever been around two women who speak the same foreign language and are under the impression that you do not? What they do is immediately start gabbing to one another in the foreign tongue at normal volume like you're fucking invisible. They leave everyone else so far out of the loop you'd think you were at your own funeral. Is that how we're behaving now in a civilized society? We just start talking shit in secret languages right in front of everyone's face? No. No, that that is not how we behave in this society, because this is a man's world and men have a little thing called common courtesy. Plus the only thing women talk about when they speak the same foreign language is The Penis. That's all women talk about when they're alone, too.

Women flaunt this lascivious behavior like it's some kind of Girl Scout merit badge. Women love being bad and crave a bad reputation. If you ever want to turn a woman from a nun into a complete nympho in like ten seconds, just tell her she looks like a "good girl." Tell her she looks like she's a girl who always plays it virtuous and never takes her top off.

Do you need a context? Don't make me laugh. Women

aren't that complex, and they never will be. Just walk up to some hot lady at a bus stop and say, "You look like a really nice girl." All aboard. Next stop: Getting Laid. Population: you.

Men speak foreign languages to get business done and to find out where things are on vacation—and also to swear. Women just learn foreign languages to talk about penises in front of people without getting caught. By letting everyone know about it, I'm giving them the best Christmas present they've ever had.

WOMEN ARE REALLY GOOD AT BEING SARCASTIC

Men are hilarious. Goddammit, we're so funny. We're so fucking funny, I'm laughing right now just thinking about how manly and funny men are.

Ha-ha!

Men joke around and we are damn good at it because it makes us feel good. Joking makes everyone feel good. It's for pleasure. But just like half of an Oreo cookie, there is a dark side to comedy. That dark side is sarcasm.

Men wield sarcasm with extreme prejudice. We line up a battalion of facts to decimate our opponents' defenses and bullshit, thereby toppling their Saddam-like statue of dignity with a pinpoint, laser-guided, cutting sarcastic remark. Women fucking suck at sarcasm. Women wielding sarcasm is like a Viking charging into battle with a giant salami. Embarassing.

One of the biggest problems with women and sarcasm is that they use it too much. Men know that overuse of sarcasm makes one look like a teenager who hasn't gotten a hand job yet and all his friends have. That's no way to look. Women look like that all the time.

Women enjoy looking ill-tempered and shrill. They think it empowers them and makes them look interesting, when they actually have nothing to offer. That's why women are sarcastic as often as possible.

Women also can't be sarcastic properly because, as usual, they don't understand what they're trying to use. Just like when they're trying to work a car or a computer or a menu, absolutely anything might happen if there isn't a man there to call the shots—anything but the correct thing, that is.

The key to sarcasm is the level of absurdity required in a given series of events that would allow the sarcastic remark to be true. Let's take this sarcastic remark as an example: *Women make great voters.*

Truly fucking absurd! But why is it sarcasm and not just wrong and dumb?

For the statement to be true, a great voter would have to be defined as someone who votes with their hormones or votes based on manic ravings they heard from their friends and didn't bother to look up afterward. That is when the sarcasm hits us right in the nuts. It turns out it was a trick all along meant as an illustration of the true nature of the female voter. Oh, what a hilarious and sarcastic thing for someone to have said. Boy, did I learn something. That's the nature of sarcasm.

MANOREXIA

Check this out. There's something called anorexia nervosa and it has been a big problem for women for decades. It hasn't been a big enough problem as far as I'm concerned, though. A woman just isn't at her best unless she's at least trying to be skinny as fuck.

All men's tastes are different and of equal value, but women's tastes for themselves are skewed like a knocked-over road sign pointing toward Fattyville. It's unhealthy, both physically and morally. It's called gluttony.

So what should women do? Stop eating? Throw up everything they eat? Both sound like good ideas to me—in moderation. But wouldn't you know it, women can't even do that right!

Anorexia is such a bunch of overblown horseshit. What's the difference between a bulimic woman and a binge-drinking frat boy? The difference is that one gets an after-school special and a boatload of sympathy, and the other gets academic probation. The reason women suffer from anorexia and bulimia isn't because of self-esteem. It's because none of them are doing it right!

Try a mouthguard, ladies. Bulimia fucks up your teeth. And how about vitamin supplements? Jesus, that's just right off the top of my head. If this book were meant for women, I could go on.

There's nothing wrong with skipping a course of frappuccinos, cupcakes, and pies. Some men in the armed forces are trained not to eat for like a week. I heard that in an Army commercial, and every time I think about it, I want to throw my next meal in the trash and kick someone's ass.

"I'll show men," say women. "Men want me to be skinny? I'll starve myself to death!"

Brilliant move, sweetheart. But that's still not going to get you pregnant.

If men had anorexia or bulimia, it would be very different. First, they would be called *manorexia* and *manlimia*. That means it's for men only. Second, *manorexia* would be when a man opted not to eat a second lunch of potato chips and beer because he was too drunk, or when he skipped breakfast because he's too fucking busy at work to fuck around with a bunch of eggs.

Manorexia would also be when you're stationed somewhere with your squadron and you have enough supplies for five days, but you've been there for eleven days, because that's how many days it's taking to get the job done. That's what happened in the Army commercial I was talking about. Goddamn if that commercial doesn't get me hard every time I see it.

There are no brochures in business school extolling the

dangers of skipping breakfast to meet a deadline and no organizations set up to spread awareness of drinking until you throw up the bag of Cheetos you ate for dinner. You can just buy another bag of Cheetos.

The Female Trinity of Wrongness

If we made a list of all the problems women have with all the things in the world, it would be longer than Santa's, and half of it would contradict the other half.

"I have problems with my self-image!"

"I hate how men always stare at my hot body!"

"Why is it that halter tops cost more than T-shirts? There's less shirt!"

It's hard to contradict yourself twice in a row and still remain wrong, but there you have it. That's the Female Trinity of Wrongness. Three separate contradicting thoughts and each one of them wronger than the last. Women are the only species in the universe able to be wrong in an infinite number of ways.

What about the problems men have with their self-image?

I'm joking! No man has ever given a shit about what he looks like. That's why we wear flannel shirts and grow beards and mustaches. Women are just silly and superficial and think they can solve problems by flushing them down the toilet in a dark bathroom. Try getting a job instead.

Anorexia is a woman's need to be loved personified. Women have no jobs or accomplishments, so not eating fills the void and is somehow more womanly than buying a shitty guitar and learning to play or volunteering at a homeless shelter. Next time you feel bad for some ninety-pound bulimic, just remember there's a little boy out there who would have been the next Einstein who just fucking died for lack of the Big Mac she just flushed.

MEN ARE NERDS

What is a nerd? I'm a man, so naturally I have all the answers.

Nerds are a lot like obscenities or pornography: You know them when you see them. For now, let's just say a nerd is certainly anyone who goes to a *Star Wars* convention and participates in dressing up like *Star Wars* characters. We could easily add being a nerd is reading about *Star Wars* conventions or telling me to fucking write about fucking *Star Wars* conventions in my new book, but let's just leave it at that.

Apparently, there are such things as *Star Wars* conventions, and apparently people dress up like *Star Wars* characters for these conventions. It's a bit like Halloween I guess, except instead of candy, you get Chewbacca merchandise? I don't know how the fuck it works.

But I do know how women work—they fuck up everything with their Aura of Ruin and their Trinity of Wrongness. The rage for women at these Star Wars conventions is to dress up like slutty versions of *Star Wars* characters. What the fuck?

I don't know what offends my man-sensibilities more in this case: the flagrant display of sexuality where it is completely inappropriate, or the lame and contrived way women choose to shit all over cherished childhood memories. Way to go, ladies. You've lowered the bar yet again.

The last thing I ever want to see is a women in a dominatrix outfit and a Darth Vader helmet. What the fuck is that? Stormtroopers don't have boobs.

Men understand what it is to be a nerd. It means being interested and committed to an idea or a set of ideas in a way some might consider fanatical. Does that sound familiar? You've probably heard of something called fucking democracy.

Democracy was founded by a bunch of nerds who were nerdy for your civil liberties, and boy were they fucking nerding it up. They drafted little nerd memos to each other called Bills of Rights and wrote secret nerd journals about voting and free trade fan fiction. That's what a man nerd is capable of: creating the best form of government in the world.

A woman nerd is capable of trouncing around in a cute outfit and getting attention she has no business getting in the real world. I wouldn't pour hot coffee on a burning female Darth Vader even if I knew the coffee guy had pissed into my coffee for some reason. I would rather drink it, piss and all.

Women's only skill is dressing slutty. Think Yoda ears on a girl in a bikini. I don't know what else, because I don't go to *Star Wars* conventions, and I never will.

THE L WORD

No matter what time of year it is, either Christmas or Valentine's Day is right around the corner. That means expensive gifts across the land are lining store shelves in wait for some lucky girl who is about to have her love purchased.

To a man, being in love is a lot like getting a promotion. It's exciting and it has the potential to improve your quality of life, but it requires that we men behave with discretion and self-respect. That's what love is to men: self-respect.

You don't see a man running out of his boss's office and spiking a stapler after getting a promotion, do you? Perhaps a man will buy a round of drinks for his buddies. That would be perfectly discreet and brimming with self-respect. Love is exactly the same. Something has happened which is good for now; maybe it will work, maybe it won't; punches will be rolled with, and a few might have to be dealt.

To a woman, being in love is a license to behave like a fucking lunatic. Men, women, children—women don't actually love any of them. They only love their precious and tacky love-trinkets, like the jewelry and bath products and gifts on which women base the foundations of a good relationship.

Women in love are like the mad inventor who never had time to start a family of his own. He was probably too busy inventing time machines and helicopters that ran on disappointment. To compensate, the aging scientist builds weird robot replicas of families. Edward Scissorhands is a good example of exactly the manner of shit women perpetrate when

they say they're in love. They just pull a bunch of fake emotions out their ass and mix them together into a big gumbo
of delusion, then they pig out on it.

Talk to a woman about love and she'll go on for hours
with nonsense and aphorisms. They're like used car sales-
men, except they're selling the same tired junk to *themselves*.

Women think about love so goddamn much that by the
time it comes around, they've trained themselves to react
like kung fu masters. Kung fu masters don't have to see
you punching them in the nuts to block it. It just happens.
Women are the same. Every signal and reaction is automatic,
and from the barroom to the bedroom they're on autopilot,
soaking in the adulation and shelling out the storybook shill.
Women don't have to learn anything about you to hop into
the love sack, they just have to hear the right code words.

Women debase themselves regularly for love. Their love
of not being wrong and their love of not having to admit the
fantasy upon which they've built their self-worth are impossible and stupid. The first step to being in love is growing
the fuck up.

DRUNK LIKE A FOX

If you've spent any amount of time in a bar or at a party,
you will find appalling the number of women who wantonly
throw themselves at you in a drunken stupor. I'm obviously
not talking about the hot women—who likely have a strong

liquor leash fastened to their necks by a caring and possessive boyfriend. I'm talking about the fatties.

And I thought fat people could hold their liquor!

Women can handle their liquor about as well as a bargain paper towel. The second they consume it, they default to ranting, stumbling harlots with a two-second fuse for erupting into hysterics. Then again, the only way to tell the difference between a drunk woman and a sober one is that the drunk will actually put out.

Women's entire lives revolve around excuses for behaving badly: PMS, pregnancy, crappy brains soaked with romantic delusions they willingly embrace at every opportunity. To women, alcohol is like the magical Giving Tree, just waiting to be pruned for excuses.

If a woman feels like letting her hair down (and by "hair" I mean "drawers"), then she turns to her best friend, Schnapps. Peach, peppermint, or Danish; she loves them all, and when she does, she gives herself a golden ticket into a wonderland of behaving terribly and "not remembering" any of it the next day.

Women's memories are funny like that. They don't work at all regularly, but then for some reason when alcohol is involved, they work even less.

Men handle alcohol just like we handle everything in life: with total class and respect. Men do not guzzle alcohol down and then throw ourselves at our father-issues like rag dolls. Men use alcohol to relax, we use it to bond, and we use it to infuse ourselves with the class we're constantly dripping with anyway. That's why men invented martinis and scotch. Those things are pure class. Women hate those drinks.

Men also use drinking to pioneer. When sober, even a man might not think something like shaving a cat is funny. That's where alcohol comes in. When properly inebriated, a man will discover that not only is shaving a cat funny, but it is so fucking funny he will probably have to buy more cats.

RUBBER DUCKY, FUCK YOU'RE SLOW

Faster means better. All men know that.

When making statements like "faster is better," all men also realize that it stands so long as quality is not compromised. If one man were to say, "These speakers would be much better if they were louder," no other man would object to that. The inherent implication is that they wouldn't be shitty with distortion.

Women are so silly and wrong that even if they were allowed to read what I just wrote, they'd still fuck it up. Ideas are more than language, and language is more than words. Women look at a forest and see a bunch of trees uncomfortably close to one another. They look at a box of Legos and see debris. They look at children and see someone to listen to their chatter instead of a future NFL quarterback.

That's why Lego makes Spaceman and Pirate sets and not Tea Party or How to Juggle Two Sugar Daddies sets.

A man has a lot of ass to kick every day, and none of it is

getting kicked in the shower. That's why men are in and out in under ten minutes. Women take like seventy minutes.

In the shower, gravity is your friend. You wash the hair; then you wash the face; then you wash your man-ass. Whatever body parts you're washing that day, gravity is your shower helper-monkey. Women, however, fight gravity just like they fight fucking everything else in their lives, biology included. Women shave their legs first. Then they wash their hair. Then they get out of the shower to get a new bar of soap, thereby getting water all the fuck over the place even though there were three perfectly good soap slivers in the shower already that could have been mashed together.

Some women paint their toenails and just sit on the toilet for like ten minutes, completely forgetting the shower is on. I guess they get confused and think they're in the rain forest or something.

If you want the experience of a woman using your bathroom, just take a bucket of water and throw it all the fuck over the place. Then drag a wet towel through your house.

MEN ARE ECO-FRIENDLIER

When you think of the term "eco-friendly," you probably think of a bunch of obnoxious women braying on endlessly with catchphrases that they could never possibly understand:

Do your part!

What the fuck does any woman know about doing her part? The bit where it's over? The bit where everyone thanks you?

When I think "eco-friendly," I think of the time a man changed the old McDonald's Styrofoam wrappers into the new 100% recycled paper—even though the old ones were cooler. I know that actually helped the problem, because it didn't involve a bunch of fatties sitting around gorging themselves on wine and chocolate, ordering hemp sweaters from thick printed paper catalogs, and dreaming about moving to Seattle.

Women are all talk and a bunch of blowhards. That's why they respond so well to that kind of shit. When you as a man are pretending to be a pompous, arrogant ass, you're speaking a language women understand. It's like barking at a dog. You don't know what you're saying, but the dog will bark back sometimes.

The only thing that's important to women and dogs is your conviction and your volume. Women take stances on all issues in exactly the same way: loud, but with no substance at all, and while pandering to the media as much as possible.

GREAT. I ALWAYS WANTED A MICKEY MOUSE TIE

This is a modern age of more sports magazines than you could read in a lifetime, services that will send you selections of exotic whiskeys year-round, and automatic pornography machines; why is it so fucking hard for women to give one good present?

They don't even have to spend their own money!

It doesn't seem like men would be better than women at giving gifts, since women are so fucking obsessed with getting gifts, but they are. Let me list the last few presents I got from women:

1. *Ankle socks*—I have never ever in my life worn this type of sock.

2. *Tag Body Spray.*

3. *A shirt with pink and lime green stripes.*

4. *A picture frame with a picture of guess who already in it.*

5. *Dove soap.*

These were things I needed about as much as I needed a broken bicycle or a reputation as the fastest cock puncher in the West, and that's exactly what I said when I opened them.

"Why didn't you just get me a broken bicycle? You could have easily found that in the trash."

Just as soon as I said it, I realized why she hadn't. Digging in the trash takes work. It takes a lot more work than walking into a Thrifty Mart and purchasing a twelve-pack of Dove soap. I could also store a broken bicycle in the trash can when I wasn't using it. Fuck, I could actually *not use* a broken bicycle. I can't not use a pack of Dove soap or a picture frame.

And why not count the picture frame and the picture it contains as two separate presents? I could then enjoy them at different times and double my appreciation. The frame I could enjoy while it held an autographed picture of Nicolas Cage on the set of *The Rock*, and the picture I could enjoy in the closet under some shit I don't care about.

Women get presents for men with one and only one thought in mind: *What's the cheapest and easiest thing to buy that will be a constant reminder of me?*

And not only a reminder to you, but also to fucking everyone in the world who happens to see it. Think you want a remote control speedboat for Christmas? I know I do. Oh, guess what? What we actually want are hideous sweaters with our wives' faces embroidered across them and nooses stitched into the collars.

KNIGHT TO PAWN FOUR. CHECK AND BULLSHIT

Wherever there is a league of sports, there is a separate and exclusive women's league to weep in its shadow. That's because a man playing a sport against a woman is like Superman playing a sport against a team of chimps wearing funny sunglasses. It's cute and hilarious, but no one would pay to watch it.

Man has proven his physical prowess over women for millions of years—even when it was completely unnecessary to do so. But it's not just our mighty strength that allows us men to soar above the earth like gods in our awe-inspiring spectacles of sport, while women stay hopelessly tethered to charity time slots. Men are also better than women at sports because men are smarter than women.

What if men invented sports that were purely mental?

What if we then called those sports chess and poker, and women fucked up at them so badly they needed their own leagues just to compete?

The Women's Chess League is not a stunt like when Andy Kaufman used to wrestle women or the time a woman played golf in the men's league and Nike again milked their biggest cash cow to date: fake female empowerment.

Women's leagues are like midgets following men around dressed up exactly like them. Women's sports are like low-income housing. Everyone hates them, and they would just disappear if the fuck wasn't subsidized out of them.

THERE'S A PARTY IN MY PANTS

I had the extreme misfortune yesterday of watching a show on MTV called *The Best Sixteenth Birthday in the World for One Hugely Spoiled Bitch*, or something like that. I don't remember what it was called exactly, but what I do remember exactly was how fucking terribly the girls on the show behaved, and how all women behave in the exact same atrocious manner.

Like everything I've ever learned as a man, the show

taught me something I already knew. Men are better than women at throwing parties, and it's not just because women's organizational skills are a clusterfuck or because they turn into raving psychos when they have to deal with the kind of stress involved in getting two dozen baked goods from the corner market and having a dress hemmed before Thursday. Men are better than women at throwing parties because women have their party attitudes backward.

When men throw a party, we make sure everyone has a good time. As long as everyone is well fed, well drunk, and well on their way home by the end of the night with a smile, it was a good party. Like the Greeks threw parties for their gods, women throw parties for themselves, and guess who's enjoying the libations? Like all the other times they've done something ordinary, women throwing parties expect worship and attention in heaps.

"Where did you get these napkin holders that also look like magicians' hats? Did you purchase them out of a catalog? Well, it really ties the whole theme together. You're so creative, and I'm so glad that eighteen-pack of Amstel Light lasted like twenty minutes! I can't wait to be impressed at how concerned you are for my well-being when I go for my car keys in three hours!"

That's the kind of shit you have to say at a woman's party if you ever expect to get invited back. When a man plans a party, he asks himself these questions and then the party planning is done:

1. Do I have a trash can full of ice and beer?

2. Do I have as many chips and hero sandwiches as will fit in the shopping cart?

LEAVE A MESSAGE AFTER THE BEEP, NOT A MONOLOGUE

Like most things, an answering machine is one thing and not a lot of other things. Like how a screwdriver is a driver of screws and not a pryer of shit out of other shit. Or how a car is not a chair, so get the fuck off of the hood no matter how cute your skirt is.

An answering machine is a machine to take your messages while you are away on man-business. It isn't a mechanical therapist for listening to ten-minute messages that have no point.

Men leave messages like they're speaking in Spanish— which they are also better at than women. In Spanish, if a question is a question, it starts with a question mark to let you know.

"Call me back. This is Bill," or "I need a ride to my car. This is Bill again."

That's how it's done correctly. Men put the purpose of the message right up front. Women leave messages in which every sentence starts with "um" or "so" or a five-second silence while they change hands to pay for their Starbucks. Fuck the other people who are waiting in line—I need to leave someone a voice mail right now!

Does any cell phone company offer a way to refuse all voice mails from women? No. That would save too many billable minutes of me deciphering what in the fuck a woman is talking about. Do I need to pick anyone up or call anyone back? Do I need to get tested for something? Is this urgent at all?

Of course it's not urgent. Women never have anything urgent to talk about until they're pregnant, and then the only thing urgent is your drinking problem.

SO, PUBLIC SPERKING—I MEAN, SPEAKING. YA KNOW?

I can count the number of great women public speakers throughout history on no hands:

Zero.

Women make lousy public speakers. They can't engage an audience, and they can't keep the attention of an audience for longer than a few minutes without relying on some kind of amateurish sexual titillation. That's why Miss Universe doesn't get to give a victory speech. It's just a wet T-shirt contest without the water and not even worth discussing.

What is worth discussing is how much better men are than women when it comes to being eloquent—lots.

To begin any public address, a man will start with a joke to warm up the crowd. It's a device that has worked *mantastically* for thousands of oratory years; from Homer to Hitler.

Right off the top, this is completely out for women. Women can't be funny, so instead of a joke, you get flummoxed babbling about statistics or milestones or other nonsense. That's exactly what a crowd of people wants to do before they've finished their first cup of coffee: fucking math.

I don't even want to get into how clumsily women throw their sentences together. If the human brain spontaneously combusted when the word "basically" was said more than a hundred times in a row, women wouldn't be allowed to get near propane. Grills would have an anti-woman warning label, which they already should have anyway.

KILLING ME SOFTLY

Since the beginning of time, man has sought to cheat Death by doing the deed himself. I'm talking about suicide.

There's a manliness to suicide you have to respect. "That'll show that bastard Death," men say. It's the way we men have lived since Mother Earth felt her first five across the eyes in the form of a plowshare.

Men are four times more likely to successfully commit suicide than women.

Women are three times more likely to attempt to commit suicide unsuccessfully than men.

Typical. You could replace the words "commit suicide" with absolutely whatever the fuck you wanted and it would still be accurate.

Men get the job done. Be it for reasons of gambling debts, existential loneliness, or simple oldness; men know how to do everything with their lives, including how to end them. Women just know how to fill out credit card applications and adopt another cat. They can't commit suicide, because they don't even know how the body works.

If you ask a man how to get in shape, he'll say, "Eat less, exercise more." It's the miracle fucking diet. Ask a woman the same question and you'll get, "Resolve your emotional issues with your mother by taking a class at the Learning Annex."

By which she means snacking on Doritos in the back of a religious studies seminar while learning about the prevalence of spirit-guides.

THAT'LL STILL LOOK HOT WHEN YOU'RE 80, DICK SAID SARCASTICALLY

When men get tattoos, they are unique and meaningful. Men get tattoos like *Where's Waldo* riding a comet across their backs, or two girls in bikinis lifting an anchor. That's awesome. How about a Chinese character that means "badass"? It probably means a bunch of other awesome shit too, because Chinese characters are complex.

When women get tattoos, it's always the same fucking thing: a rose on her boob, which you're not supposed to look at, or some kind of a target above the ass. If man tattoos were as predictable and transparent as women's, every man would have a giant dollar sign tattooed on his chest with an arrow pointing to his cock.

Fortunately for everyone, men have a little thing called class.

Tattoos have been man's domain all the way back to a time when men were out hunting and gathering while women soaked their feet.

I imagine men invented tattoos in order to proudly display how many woolly mammoths they'd slain in battle with their bare hands. How many woolly mammoths has a woman ever killed? None. She likes Tinker Bell, though. For fuck's sake, does she ever like Tinker Bell!

Man tattoos are statements. "Where's Waldo? He's right the fuck here!" That's a statement. It doesn't get any more manly than a comet. Unless there are reverse comets out there where the tail sticks out in front. That's another subtle penis joke.

What does some stupid, pseudo-Indian design on a woman's lower back say? "I'm in touch with the spirit of nature?" Probably not. It doesn't say "I'm spiritual." It doesn't even say "Look at my lower back" or "I need loads of attention."

It says "I'm just decoration."

Women don't have enough philosophy or personality on which to base a tattoo. That's why they suck at getting them. That's also why women love Hallmark so fucking much. Hallmark is all a bunch of prepackaged, corny bullshit, and yet it defines the essence of a woman's being in two sentences on a porcelain figurine with oversize eyes or a 4×6 inch reprint of a Monet.

Women *are* Hallmark. They're way overpriced, none of them do a goddamn thing, and someone's going to get hurt feelings if you chuck them out before the week is up.

THE BOOB TUBE

Like everything else, TV was invented by a man. His name was Philo T. Farnsworth. Next, the invention was proliferated by other men—businessmen who reinvented paradigms and thought so far outside the box that my man-senses quake at the mention of it. Men are good at both inventing things and proliferating them, but that's not what I want to talk about here.

Men are also better than women at watching television. Television is a good fit with men in the same way kicks in the ass are a good fit with women in college, who all think they have a fucking opinion on everything.

Television is about relaxing and feeling good, but then it can also be about spreading information about wrestling. From your ABCs to your HSQs (Hitlers, Sharks, and Queer Eyes), television teaches as it entertains. Like men, television is versatile as shit.

Women are not versatile and only watch shows their friends watch or shows that are extremely popular. Men, as the pioneers we are, will devote several hours a day to exploring the smorgasbord that is cable programming.

If there's something good out there in TV Land, a man will find it and watch the shit out of it. Then he'll share it with the world. That's why Santa Claus is a man. If Santa were a woman, she would keep all the toys in a big warehouse and guilt-trip the elves for not convincing her she didn't have a fat ass.

Women also don't watch commercials. The second a commercial starts, all women in the room start yammering.

Some women even mute the commercials! In what fucked reality would I rather hear a woman think out loud than listen to thirty seconds of the Who rocking out, set to some badass dude driving a badass car?

ANIMAL FARM

Zoos have been around for as long as animals. That is a long fucking time. And in this time, men have enjoyed zoos to the fullest. We have taken leisurely strolls around them. Some of us have been fortunate enough to drink several beers in them, because some of us have been to London where you can do that.

London is a manly place. Getting drunk at the zoo is economical and relaxing to the mind and body. Men can relax without blowing a week's paycheck at some fancy day spa.

Recently at the zoo, I had the misfortune of getting stuck among a group of elementary schoolgirls near the penguin compound. This is what I heard:

"I want one of those!"

"I want two of those!"

"Why can't I have one of those?"

Jesus Christ. The zoo is not *Pokémon*, and it's not a pet store. Seeing the blatantly female traits of greed and avarice showing so clearly in girls as young as ten and eleven made me too sick to eat my churro.

As divine providence would have it, while in the snake house, I encountered a group of young schoolmen out on their field man-trip.

"Why do snakes stick out their tongues?"

"Why don't snakes blink?"

"If a snake ate its tail, would it disappear?"

I had to sit down for a moment, because the weight of what I was seeing and hearing was hitting me like a ton of bricks. All on their own, these young men were learning. They were analyzing and putting together their surroundings and forming new ideas. These little schoolmen were like human garbage disposals, except working in the opposite way—the way that makes sense with what I'm talking about.

Sometimes I fear that one day, state-mandated equality will dash our civilization to pieces like a great tidal wave of horseshit. Not so. If the face of the earth were wiped clean of adults tomorrow and the children had to pick up from scratch, we'd be right back on track again in five minutes. Maybe even faster, because little girls haven't learned about feminism by the age of ten and eleven, they've just learned how to want things so much they can cry from it. Oh, wait.

I also scored myself sixty ounces of man-points by sneaking a four-pack of Boddingtons into the zoo in my pants. I don't want to give away all of my secrets in this book, but here's a tip for you crafty men:

If someone gets caught hiding two Coronas in his pocket, what are the odds he's got a four-pack of Boddingtons in his pants?

Think about it, because security guards never do.

WOMEN SUCK AT BOARD GAMES

Women need a practice round for everything. They need a practice marriage, they need a practice job, they need an entire practice life to get all the kinks out. Otherwise, you just have a grown-up child-woman wandering around aimlessly chucking money all over the board when everyone's just waiting for her to roll the fucking dice or start crying because you're being condescending. No shit I'm being condescending. The card said move your piece back three spaces. How the fuck am I supposed to explain that in a noncondescending way?

All board games come with fucked instructions and reading them is a waste of time. Did you know the $500 bonus for landing on Free Parking isn't even in the Monopoly instructions? You're also only allowed to have one hotel per property. And no one is allowed to hand everyone else hundreds out of the bank when someone goes to take a shit. That doesn't sound like any kind of Monopoly I want to play.

Instructions don't matter. All games should be played the same way: *manily*.

Do you know what the purpose of board games is?

The purpose of board games is to fuck around and get drunk with your buddies. So I can think of twenty-six points worth of *P* words. Did I win any money? No? Then who the fuck cares?

Women. Without careers, aspirations, or accolades, those twenty-six points are all they have.

ONE CHEESEBURGER, HOLD THE JIBBER-JABBER

If you're pressed for time on your lunch break and you walk into your favorite restaurant only to see a team of broads manning the tills, just turn around and walk the fuck out, because you are definitely going to be late for work.

From Barclay's to McDonald's, women serve customers about as well as they serve pithy remarks: poorly. Their heads are full of ground-up lollipops. Over ten thousand years, men have built a thriving global economy that kicks the asses of hunger and disease all over the world. Women, on the other hand, have what is called a "nesting" instinct. "Nesting" is just a nice name we've given to something lame that women do. Just like "empowered," which is a nice name we have for women who are 25% slutty, 75% bitchy, and 100% incompetent.

KEEP THE CAMPING TO PURSE SALES

Women are so bad at camping, there's almost nothing as unpleasant as camping with a woman.

Except camping with two women.

Like a snake shedding its skin, women shirk the equality ruse when it suits them. In the cases of camping, construction working, or cigarette smoking worth a fuck, women play the princess card faster and more dextrously than Tommy played pinball.

The dirt and infrequent showers have nothing to do with why women hate camping. Imagine this if you will:

You've accidentally locked yourself inside a shitty motel room in some hick town, because you dropped a suitcase on the doorknob and broke it off. The only thing in the room for entertainment is a television set. Oh, great. It turns out that some prick broke the television set. It looks like all you have for your entertainment is your massive male brain.

Sound like fun? Absolutely.

But if you weren't a man, that kind of thing would reduce you to a babbling, neurotic mess within an hour. Women behave like shrill disasters when they are taken camping, because a woman's mind isn't the splendorous and orgiastic wonderland of adventure that is a man's. A woman's head is a Podunk, no-doorknob motel room, and her mind is a broken television set.

How many women philosophers have there been? None. Not only do philosophers have to understand what they're saying, but they also have to be alone with their thoughts for longer than four seconds without calling their girlfriends to gossip.

To all the young men out there who are dreaming of a woman who can go camping with them or some other crazy shit—like go drinking, stay out late, or play video games— why hold out for just one? Why not hold out for two? How about a baker's dozen of unreasonably perfect women who can express themselves without being bitches? The sky's the limit in fantasyland where a woman can go camping without making everyone fucking miserable with her pissy attitude.

That's the same reason women will never go to the moon.

WOMEN PARKING? FUCK OFF

Being a man is getting out of your car, looking at your fucked-up parking job, and then getting back in your car and parking correctly.

Being a woman is pulling up to the curb like a drunken teenager, mashing your tire against the concrete like you're humping a doorknob, and then getting out of your car while on a cell phone and letting someone else be inconvenienced by the whole shit.

Think of driving like fucking. Men initiate it, do all the work, and let everyone know when it's done. Who gives a fuck when women think it's done? That's like a bus driver going around town telling banks it's time to close up for the day.

A bus driver knows dick about banking, and that's exactly what women know about driving and also parking. Have you ever watched a woman park? It hurts me in my balls. As a man, I have these things called testicles, and they hurt when I have to watch a woman drive a sixty-thousand-dollar something in between two other sixty-thousand-dollar somethings. I can't explain it, I'm just telling you where it hurts and when.

I don't know where in the fuck women get the idea that they should drive. They can't clear the very first hurdle, which is pulling out of and pulling into a parking spot. The big cement thing that stops your car from rolling into the beauty parlor, which is commonly called a curb, is just a suggestion. It is not an embankment to use like your fat friend as you stumble to your car after last call.

THE SECOND STEP IS ADMITTING IT

Unlike women, men can be a whole shitload of things over the course of our lives, and we can be these things without relying on government quotas or miniskirts.

Men can excel in academia, we can also become top businessmen in sharp-looking suits, or we can simply be good parents. That's also a noble aim. Who knows, your man-child might become a brilliant scientist or a real estate mogul. Then all that parenting doesn't seem like such a waste of time, does it?

While managing so many responsibilities, we men from time to time can also be wrong. Men can't be wrong in the way women are wrong, though. The way a man can be wrong is like placing the fork and knife on the wrong sides of the plate. Who cares, you're still going to eat without getting food all over your hands. The way women are wrong is by throwing the silverware in the pool, setting dinner on fire, and then playing the pregnant card like it's Uno.

It's a widely bullshat myth that men can't admit they're wrong. Men admit they're wrong all the fucking time. Men cross the goal line of wrong and spike the apology ball right into life's face by fixing our fucking mistakes. We don't sit around crying and blowing snot everywhere.

Men admit we're wrong and then we make it right. I've bought so many people new cell phones that I'm not even sure I ruined all of them. Everyone says I did though, so fuck it. I guess I'm the asshole.

To a woman, being wrong is a one- out of two-step process. The first step is the fuckup, and women certainly fuck up. From worthless history degrees to mixed signals to prison pen pals, women are ten fuckups in a two fuckup sack. The second step is admitting it. And that's where a woman's journey of wrong ends in a river of tears and snot and attention.

Women fuck up, and some man comes along and unfucks it up before she's done bawling. When she opens her eyes, the fuckup has evaporated so quickly her brain has been tricked into thinking it never happened. Film projectors work on the same principle. Women's fuckups are the blank spots between the frames in the illusion that is their lives.

Fuck, I've just blown my own mind.

I'LL TAKE HOW TO FUCK MY LIFE UP FOR 1000, ALEX

What do you know, it's the Daily Double.

The answer is: It's the easiest possible way to fuck up your life.

Everyone knows the saying "Don't let a bald man cut your hair." It works as a saying because the guy's bald and that's funny first of all, but it's also insightful and makes a good point.

Here's a similar saying that I'm about to invent using the same formula of taking someone with no frame of reference and no fucking clue at all and making them do something they shouldn't ever in a million years be doing, because only massive failure could result.

Are you ready for it?

Never ask a woman for relationship advice.

Ask a woman for legal advice before you ask her for relationship advice. Then ask her for a GET OUT OF JAIL FREE card, because that's where you're going, jackass. Women have no clue how to behave in a relationship. They don't know how to start a relationship, and they don't know how to end one. That knowledge exceeds the clearance limit posted on the entrance.

Women can't even manage a career and a relationship at the same time. For fuck's sake, men have been managing relationships and careers since the first human being got hungry for the first time. Men didn't look at each other and say, "Well, how the fuck are we supposed to have sex with all these women if we're also hungry? I give up!"

There's no saying that goes "Don't let lice cut your hair." That's gross and no one would ever say it. It's a more accurate comparison though—letting lice cut your hair is like listening to a woman tell you how to fix a relationship.

Observe for yourself. Fabricate a relationship problem, a simple relationship problem with a simple solution. Then find your nearest woman and ask for help. If she's not a family member, she'll most likely try to have sex with you on the spot. Women are conditioned like dogs to respond sexually to any of the following words: communication, respect, support, nurturing, Napa Valley.

Here's an example of a simple relationship problem, in case you have better things to do with your time than sit around and think up imaginary problems. That's what mothers do all day, which is why their work is never done.

My spouse has a heroin problem, what should I do?

If you think making women spell is hilarious, wait until you get rained on by a tornado of the stupidest fucking brainstorm ever said. Women are God's Mad Libs. The sentences fly and it's wacky fun and silliness for everyone, so long as your idea of wacky fun and silliness contains the words "true love" and "soul mate" about a hundred fucking times. Women drape those asinine concepts like Christmas lights around any mound of bullshit. It doesn't matter how often they call it a Christmas tree, Santa's not eating cookies and milk from under a pile of shit.

Any man asked that question won't even answer. He'll just take you to the bus station and buy you a one-way ticket to anywhere you want to go. Women don't realize that when you're stuck between a rock and a fucked place, you need to cut the anchor cable and get the fuck out. Just because the ship is sinking doesn't mean the life preservers have to go down with it.

So, the easiest possible way to fuck up your life:

What is, "asking a woman for advice," Alex?"

Luckily, I wagered all of my man-points for a true Daily Double.

SPEAKING OF *JEOPARDY!*, WOMEN SUCK AT *JEOPARDY!*

Last time I saw a woman playing *Jeopardy!*, she didn't even make it to the final round, because she had fucked up all her money.

I felt bad for her in a way, but I felt even worse for myself for being deprived the evening of *mantertainment* that only a cutthroat three-way round of *Jeopardy!* can provide. Watching *Jeopardy!* when a woman is playing isn't three-way or cutthroat at all. It's just another ridiculous trouncing of women by men and another day in a gender war where one side is armed with obnoxious opinions and the other side with nukes. *Jeopardy!* with a woman is like getting a three-chambered peanut with only two nuts inside.

Dick Takes on Jeopardy

I have calculated, statistically, the role women have played in the *Jeopardy!* Tournament of Champions from available data between 1985 and 2000. The *Jeopardy!* Tournament of Champions is like the World Cup of knowing things. If you want to find out who is the best slam-dunker, you have a slam-dunk contest. If you want to find out who is smarter, men or women, then you have a knowing-shit contest. What's so hard about that? You can also have a Change Your Own Fucking Tire contest, but what's the point? Women think "Lefty Loosey" is a guy they blew in high school.

Women make up 13 percent of Jeopardy! *champions.*
Women make up 16 percent of Jeopardy! *champion finalists.*

Out of the two times women have won the *Jeopardy!* Tournament of Champions, one was by a single dollar, so that doesn't even count. I once found ten dollars just lying in the street, and I don't know what element soap is made out of or what ancient civilization invented yeast.

The answer is: This is the same as your cock turning into a raspberry scone.

What are, "the odds of a woman being a *Jeopardy!* champion, Alex?" Or is the *Jeopardy!* part even necessary—should it just be "champion"?

Again I wagered all my man-points. I'm on fire!

	quarterfinalist women	semifinalist women	finalist women	female winner?
1985	3/15	1/9	0/3	fuck no
1986	0/15	0/9	0/3	fuck no
1987	0/15	0/9	0/3	fuck no
1988	4/15	3/9	1/3	last place
1989	3/15	2/9	0/3	fuck no
1990	2/15	1/9	0/3	fuck no
1991	3/15	1/9	0/3	fuck no
1992	2/15	2/9	0/3	fuck no
1993	6/15*	4/9*	2/3	fuck no**
1994	3/15	2/9	1/3	by one dollar
1995	1/15	0/9	0/3	fuck no
1996	N/A	3/9	0/3	fuck no
1997	5*/15*	4/9*	1/3	fuck no
1999	4/15	1/9	1/3	last place
2000	6/15*	2/9	1/3	barely
	20%	19%	16%	13%

* Two women were in the same game.
** One man is all it takes.

WOMEN ARE A DRAG, MAN. DRAG MAN?

Tootsie was a pretty good movie. So were *Mrs. Doubtfire* and *Ladybugs*. What did these movies have in common? Men in drag.

Monty Python also features men in drag. Those guys are hilarious.

I've seen women in drag before, and none of them were good entertainment. You can always spot a woman in drag, because women both are shitty actors and don't know dick about men or how to act like them. Usually, you can see women dressing up like men when a couple of "lesbians" want to hit the town and pretend one of them is a guy and the other could get a second look from anything.

But sometimes it's just some really ugly woman who I thought was trying to look like a man. I've fallen for that one a few times. I felt bad at first, but I don't see how the fuck it's my fault. If you're a woman and you look like a man, wear a little bow in your hair or something. Ms. Pac-Man never gets mistaken for her husband.

Have you ever heard the saying "Don't judge a man until you've walked a mile in his shoes"? Well I have, and what that saying means is that men do something called walking. You can never walk a mile in a woman's shoes, because all women do all day is shop and get their asses kissed. That's like a half mile of walking at most! There's nothing else to a woman's entire life. Even the ones who have a job just get their asses kissed twice as much for all the shopping they're not doing.

All day, every day, it's wake up, get your ass kissed for eight hours, then go shopping and probably throw in some more ass-kissing before not putting out for the night. What the Christ is there to understand about that?

Men are better than women at cross-dressing. We just have to empty our heads to act like women. Women would have to cram twenty pounds of brain into their ten-pound skulls. Unlikely.

WHAT DO THE SUPER BOWL, BOXING, AND WRESTLING HAVE IN COMMON?

Men do everything in one of two ways. We either do things as hard and as fast as possible, like a Corvette with Jimmy Page airbrushed onto the hood—awesome; or we do them not at all.

Men wear jewelry in the same way we celebrate sons who are superb athletes or the way we have midlife crises. When it's happening, everyone knows it and everyone better fucking recognize it as a big deal. The World Wrestling Entertainment championship title belt weighs over six pounds. Deal with that.

What comes to mind when you think of a ring? Probably some chintzy little strip of gold with a diamond and a 150-pound anchor attached to it sinking you into a pit of despair. The anchor is a metaphor for the woman wearing it.

Women take something stunning and rare and awesome

like gold and rubies and ruin them with ostentatious con-
sumerism. That's why you don't see men drooling over
engagement rings at the mall come February 1st. Men, by
nature, are not attracted to ostentation.

When I think of a man-ring, I think of nothing less than
the ultimate in class and refinement, times two.

What do the Super Bowl, boxing, and wrestling have
in common? Enormous men with bad attitudes and stately
rings worth more than your ass. That's the man-side of
jewelry.

CHAPTER 3

Myths and Lores

When writing this book, I heard some horseshit from people about how I was wrong. Copernicus heard a lot of horseshit about how he was wrong too. So did Jesus.

I've compiled this section to debunk some of the most subversive female myths perpetrated on the male sex.

CHILDBIRTH IS NOT A BIG DEAL

A woman having babies is like an octopus shooting ink at a hungry shark. Except this octopus has six tentacles in the shark's wallet and also whore paint all over its face.

Please allow me to quote from three billion of the worst writers in the world today:

"*You men think you're so tough? Try pushing something the size of a watermelon out a hole the size of a lemon which is also called your vagina!*"—*Every woman in the world*

A classy, but inaccurate, depiction of childbirth.

Childbirth, whether it's completely disgusting or not, is a beautiful thing. In the case of baby boys being born, you could be witnessing the first breaths of the next Picasso or Pavarotti. In the case of baby women, you're witnessing something special too, probably. The point is, as a man I would never sink so low as to equate the act of childbirth to some perverse squishing of produce through holes the size of other produce. Is this human life we're talking about, or a fruit salad?

A baby is not even the size of a watermelon. It's more like the size of a large cantaloupe. Have I ever squeezed something the size of a large cantaloupe through something the size of a regular-size cantaloupe? Believe me, I have.

It's called putting on my undershirt. I don't hear my undershirt complaining about my head being the size of a watermelon, which it isn't, but it is bigger than my shirt's neck hole.

Today's modern mother is so doped up on morphine and attention that she mistakes her husband for an orderly. Men in the Napoleonic Age got their legs and arms cut off with no anesthetic and gangrenous saws. Where's your cute fruit analogy now? Have you ever had a leg the size of a giant zucchini cut in half by a carrot which was a rusty saw? That's man-pain.

I, DICK MASTERSON, JUST REPEALED THE 19TH AMENDMENT

A lot of men (and women looking to get laid) ask me why women have the right to vote. And since they very much do have it, why hasn't some kind of enormous, planet-size croquet mallet smashed the earth into the sun?

The earth is in such good condition because women actually don't have the right to vote. They never have had it, and they never will.

Recently, I was watching an attractive woman attempt to convince her dog to sit down, because she wanted it to do so. It was no surprise to me that an attractive woman couldn't do something. Attractive women can't do anything. That's why women are so proud of being stupid. Stupidity in women is directly proportional to their attractiveness. No man would ever sit an attractive woman down and say, "You don't know a goddamn thing, so shut the fuck up." Attractive women don't deserve that, and men have a little thing called sensitivity, especially when it comes to a nice ass.

When we tell a dog to sit, it sits the fuck down. That's what dogs do, because they instinctively know their place. The dog hears the command and then obeys. You can call that a decision if you want, but that doesn't make it one.

Women don't have any powers of voting, married men just get an extra vote. Men with girlfriends get an extra vote. Fathers with fat daughters get as many extra votes as they can afford cheesecakes, and I bet that's a fucking lot, because cheesecake is cheap when you buy it in bulk.

It's not that dogs have the option of eating potato chips off the ground, it's that men with dogs have an easy way to clean their kitchen floors—which is what women should be doing instead of voting.

WOMEN HATE NICE GUYS? I DON'T THINK SO

Women hate nice guys? That's stupider than *The Vagina Monologues*. Women love nice guys!

Just ask them:

When your car was stalled in the middle of a busy inter-section, who helped you push it across? A nice guy. When you had something heavy that needed dumping behind a 7-Eleven, like a couch or a fat roommate who passed out drunk in your backseat because she was trying way too hard to impress all of her whore friends, who helped you chuck it?

It was a nice guy.

Has a man ever eaten half of your pizza and then made you play ten minutes of "I'm too stupid to do math" before chipping in because *Cosmo* said that was sexy? Fuck no. That's one of the most irritating games in the world, and men don't propagate that manner of shit. If he did do it, though, it was probably extremely funny.

In life, there is no struggle where a man won't lend a man-hand. Men will even help women, which is the biggest testament of all to our undeniable niceness. A woman will never offer any kind of gratitude for services rendered. Any time a man helps a woman, he's pretty much doing it for nothing. She'll just stand there clumsily with her uncharged cell phone explaining ad naseum how life did not prepare her for whatever it was that needed doing—as if that weren't already obvious.

WOMEN ARE SO ANTI-GAY IT'S NOT EVEN FUNNY

I was walking to the store yesterday, smoking a giant Cuban cigar as I like to do on days that end in "day," and on the way, I passed a woman shouting at her dog who had wandered off and was ferreting through someone's trash.

Being the helpful man I am, I succinctly explained to the woman that the dog was not of the capacity to understand her position on the matter and that this is one of the reasons the city considers it in everyone's best interests for dogs to be kept on a leash; it's to prevent exactly this kind of failure.

The woman responded in a crass way, which I'm not going to repeat here, because it was of a nature hateful to homosexuals. Then she stormed off. I found myself asking one question:

Why do all women hate gays so much?

Women sling homosexual insults at men with the fervor and intensity of a wolf chewing a beehive. They practically spit all over themselves when they get a chance to snarl some anti-gay epithet at a man. It's disgusting.

Also, when I say "homosexual," I obviously mean gay men. Gay women, or "lesbians," are faking it. You can tell because they're as loud as possible about their sexual proclivities at all times, just like how the mischievous schoolboy who insists he doesn't cheat at Monopoly is actually a huge liar and cheater. "Lesbians" just want attention, a way to define themselves other than "failure," and to get back at their parents for clothing and sheltering them for twenty-six years.

Then, in an act of mind-numbing duplicity, women claim as loudly as possible that gays are the greatest things since sliced bread. But listen to their reasons: because gays shop and gays listen.

Listen? Women know as much about listening as asses know about playing the flute.

When they're not shaming gays behind their backs with anachronistic slanders, what women actually want to do with gays is make them sit through endless tirades of nonsensical blubbering, without ever having to return the favor.

WOMEN HATE BABIES

Remember that book Hillary Clinton wrote called *It Takes a Village to Raise a Child*? I don't know if that was the exact title, and I don't care. The point of it was: Women can't raise children on their own.

Remember that movie *Three Men and a Baby*? I do remember that title exactly, because that was a good fucking movie.

Three men is less than a village of women. What we learned in *Three Men and a Baby,* and to a lesser extent in *Three Men and a Little Lady*, is that men can raise children, work full-time jobs, maintain hobbies like drinking and bowling, and all the while still have time to chase tail and conquer hubris.

Women hate babies and children. One good way to know if you've gotten under a woman's skin is if she's speaking to you like a child. When women are yelling and screaming, that's about a 5 on my Feminine Anger and Rage Tirade scale, created by me, Dick Masterson.

A 1 on the FART scale is the silent treatment. That lasts for about a week, until she figures out silence is the dumbest way on earth to show a man you're upset with him. Shutting the fuck up around a man is like giving him ten blow jobs at the same time. Happy birthday!

Level 2 is when a woman is talking to you like a child, which means patronizingly and almost giddy with a repressed psycho-mania. That's when you know you've pissed her off, because women treat people they hate the same way they treat children, which they obviously also hate.

THE COW SAYS . . .

We've all heard "hell hath no fury like a woman scorned."

That's a fucking myth.

Remember when everyone was going on and on about how great Krispy Kreme doughnuts were? You couldn't make it from your car to your desk without hearing about how they melt in your mouth or a debate about the exact amount of time you should microwave a box of them before gorging. Krispy Kremes are good, but they're just fucking donuts. Just like women and their scorn. A woman may get pretty pissed off. Shit, women get pissed off all the time. Female anger is the weather vane of truth, and we men can be some truthful motherfuckers. But in the end, she's just a woman. What could she possibly do?

In hell, you get hot pokers shoved in your ass. The worst thing a woman can do is make all her friends want to fuck you. When a woman gets bent out of shape, the first thing she does is clam up like she knows what's good for her. Now, why is she doing this? Is it to think for a moment about whatever horrible thing she's just done or said? Or is it to reflect on her past transgressions that might have led to the current situation? Maybe to prepare an apology?

Don't be silly. Women are only quiet out of spite.

The most powerful thing a scorned woman can do is give you the silent treatment. Fuck, I've been putting that on my Christmas list since I was twelve. If anyone out there has done anything to piss a woman off, please feel free to blame it on me. That way, in the unlikely event that I run into this woman, we'll already be on not-speaking terms. Fucking perfect.

An afternoon of no complaining is not how the Bible describes hell's fury.

A woman's scorn is also telling all her friends you're an asshole. You know what? I'll just give you the whole FART Scale.

Dick Masterson's Feminine Anger and Rage Tirade Scale
1. The silent treatment
2. Patronizing you the same way her mother does to her, which she hates
3. Loud talking to her mother on the phone in the same room as you
4. Not shaving
5. Headaches
6. "I'm not sure if I remembered to take my pill today."
7. Telling all her friends you're an asshole
8. Cockteasing at work
9. Anorexia
10. Bulimia

Next time a woman is pissed off at you, use that list to see how truthful you're being on a scale of 1 to 10. And always remember: You're a man; you didn't do anything wrong.

Even when asked to, men cannot fuck up on par with a woman. It's like asking a perfectly literate person to suddenly not be able to read. Try as they might, a STOP sign will never look like a jumble of monkey shit.

Sayings like "hell hath no fury like a woman scorned," are fabrications meant to frighten children into respecting something that doesn't exist. Scorning women is like masturbating. It's fun, there are always new and interesting ways to do it, and there are no consequences. You're not going to go blind. She's not going to drive your car off a cliff or fuck up your credit. Do it as much as you want, just try to keep it out of the workplace.

See, it *is* just like masturbation.

WOMEN ARE WILD FOR WOMBS!

Women and their aimless prattlings are like Chinese people in China. There're like a billion of them, there're new ones every day, and you'll never be able to count them all.

If you were going to count them, you would have to start with this one:

Women make up for their constant drain on both society and everyone's patience because they can have babies.

Is this opposite day? Yes!

If having a baby made up for any kind of shit, then every man in the world could just roll a piano down the street instead of paying his taxes for the year.

This mythical, unthinking man would say, "Hey, I took a shitload of resources from everyone else in the form of blocking roads and noise pollution. But instead of producing anything for others to enjoy, I'm just going to roll this thing down the street in a totally irresponsible way and let everyone else deal with it."

Caring for babies is the easiest job in the world. That's why it doesn't pay shit. It's the only task a human being has never had to learn. Well, that and how to shit.

Women can have babies. Great. That doesn't make women any more equal to men than they weren't already. It just makes them more dangerous. Dangerous like a kid with a hockey stick and a blindfold who thinks he's in a piñata store.

For anyone who doesn't know what a piñata store is, it would make the kid run around like crazy and bash the shit out of everything with absolutely no regard for consequences—or your nuts.

MANGINAS ARE MY HERO

Male feminists, or "manginas" as they prefer to be called, are so misogynistic they make Andrew Dice Clay look like The Little Mermaid. The Little Mermaid is the seashell-on-the-boobs cartoon character from Disney.

Not all men have money, good looks, talent, wit, charm, charisma, interesting stories, cultural insights, skills, athletic abilities, political acumen, macho attitudes, an ability to eat an inhuman amount of food or other nontoxic products, a sense of style, an easygoing demeanor, video games, a sweet car, a spa, or an in-depth knowledge of everything. All men, however, are still men. That means they need to get laid and will always find a way.

How do these other men attract women, then? I'll tell you how—by taking charge where women have failed for the last thirty years: by being feminists.

Manginas are my heroes. They fight the fight that women declared for absolutely no reason and then completely failed at. Who else but a man could convince a woman that being a male feminist is not only possible, but also not the most chauvinistic thing anyone has ever done in the history of the world?

I'll tell you who, fucking no one! But men have done that shit. Men are like hypnosis masters when it comes to telling women what they want and what they should think about everything. Manginas are the biggest and most ingenious misogynists.

It's perfectly natural and perfectly manly for a man to stoop so low as to cheapen his entire gender just to get laid. Men don't need a collective pat on the ass for everything we do in life. We're born with dicks and dignity, and neither can be taken away. We don't need a sash that counts up all our achievements and chafes our necks. That's for Girl Scouts, and the only thing I want to know about Girl Scouts is when they sell their cookies.

On a personal note, I have nothing against misogynism, or whatever it's called. I wouldn't call myself a misogynist, but that's a little like not calling a square a rectangle.

Manginas are some of the manliest men on earth, because they know deep down within their stomachs that women can't stand up for themselves without a hand firmly supporting them by the ass. It's a throwback to chivalry that says, "Sweetheart, if you want anyone to take your rights seriously, shut up and let a man do the talking."

LESBIANS ARE FUCKING FAKING IT

Women doing anything is like using bottle rockets to change the channel when your remote runs out of batteries. You aim the bottle rocket to hit the Channel Up button ten feet away, but you know exactly what it's going to do. It's going to go shooting off in flames wherever the fuck it wants to go at random levels of ferocity and with no fucking point. That's also women when it comes to being gay.

Do you know how many women are not "lesbians"? Zero women are not "lesbians." Don't bother asking them, because all women lie about it unless they're on the radio. The point is, all women have had one or several experiences with a member of the same sex. Or they have had a fantasy about doing so, and that makes them gay. That makes all women "lesbians" and no women "lesbians."

In a "lesbian relationship," no matter how easy the question is, a woman has to answer it. That is fucked. That's probably also why "lesbians" are so fucking in love with mass transit.

No relationship can be built on the decisions of women. Everyone knows that. All the governments and all the religious texts in history have known that. Fakers.

TALK IS CHEAP

As a man, you may have heard this saying:

"Talk is cheap."

Well, it is.

You may also have heard this saying:

"One man felt smart. Two men felt smart. Three men smelt fart."

That's true, as well.

Talk is cheap as dirt and not worth fuck-all. That's why women do so much of it and take it so fucking seriously.

As men, our days consist entirely of actions. We go to work, we make deals, we have meetings. Goddammit, we *do*, and we do like motherfuckers. Women just talk endlessly. That doesn't make you a good communicator, it makes you a broken Teddy Ruxpin.

A picture is worth a thousand words, because it's a picture

of actions that are going on. How about "one in the hand is worth two in the bush"? The action of handing something makes it worth more than just sitting around talking about two things in a bush. Who the fuck cares about a bush?

Women do. They have no actions in their lives, and they have no philosophy. The only thing women have is taking everything way the fuck too seriously.

THERE IS NO DOUBLE STANDARD

"It's okay for men to sleep around, but when women do it, they're called sluts!"

Man, do I hate talking to women. Talking to women is like strolling around in an elephant pen with a blindfold on. At any moment, you could step in a shit the size of a duffel bag.

"That's called a double standard!"

That's called a double bullshit. It's not okay for men to sleep around. Sleeping around as a man means sleeping with a lot of uggos and fatties. That's a major loss of man-points. And men don't give half a shit if women sleep around, unless we're talking about our daughters, sisters, or mothers. Then it reflects poorly on us.

As usual, when women are talking about sex, they're talking only about themselves.

Women love a man-whore like they love oxygen. Telling a woman you've slept with a hundred babes is the best pickup line in the world. And the only reason women think it's not okay for them to sleep around is because women will believe anything men tell them to believe.

It's not okay for women to sleep around.

I've never done this with anyone else.

I totally respect you.

Don't make me laugh. Those are obvious lies. Respect is earned. No woman has ever earned anything in her life. Women are bought and paid for, which is why they respond so well to being propositioned:

"Would you like to go to dinner?"

"I'd love to."

That's because you're a prostitute. And the women who eat a free meal and then skip out on the requisite sex aren't crafty or empowered, they're just bad whores lousing everything up for the good whores. Once the payment takes place, you're guilty. Don't believe me? Go ask a fucking cop. How's that for a double standard?

SPORTS ARE A WOMAN'S BEST FRIENDS. SHE HATES THEM

Think you won the lottery because your woman likes sports? Think again, all women fucking hate sports. The only thing she likes is tricking you by pretending she loves something that she doesn't. That's also why she "loves" sex.

Let me tell you a story about the first primitive man. One primitive day, the first primitive man said to himself,

"Fuck! Woman are annoying." Then he made a crude cave-man-type sign that said, NO WOMEN ALLOWED IN THIS CAVE TODAY. That's when the first primitive man found himself ass-deep in women.

Women have no respect for anything, least of all themselves. And they especially have no respect for sports.

Women who claim to be interested in sports are frauds and lying to get attention. And when I say "sports," I mean baseball and football and soccer and things played by men. Girl-soccer, girl-hockey, and softball played without a keg on second base, are not sports.

Strike One

99 percent of women haven't gotten off their asses since before puberty. At the age of twelve, women give up all physical activity and begin a long life of posturing on comfy ottomans while slinging catty remarks at one another. When it comes to sports, they have absolutely no frame of reference.

Strike Two

You can't be an alcoholic unless you drink by yourself. The same is true for being a sports fan. It's great to scream and cheer at the bar in a low-cut top so a hundred guys know you're there, but has any woman ever had a San Jose Sharks logo on her underwear without anyone else knowing about it? No.

Strike Three

Listen to a woman after her favorite sports team has won the game.

"They won!"

They? What the fuck *they*?

"We won!" is how a man says it.

We won. That's why women hate sports.

DOES THIS GIRLFRIEND COME WITH A GIFT RECEIPT?

Women love shopping as much as men love not shopping. You can tell because everything in the world of wares caters to a woman's sensibilities. Walk into a department store and see for yourself. Do you see any signs anywhere? Do you see a giant neon sign that says: BATHROOMS ARE RIGHT THE FUCK HERE!? There's also no alcohol and no one watching all those fucking rotten kids running around like they own the place.

Women hate signs and booze and kids being well-behaved.

The whole process of shopping is engineered to leave you drained, late, and feeling like you've accomplished something, when in fact all you did was return some shitty presents.

Women love shopping for the same reason they love

talking: It wastes their time. That's why shopping malls are built like casinos. There are no landmarks, and there's no escape. It's like being trapped in a half-finished M. C. Escher drawing where someone forgot to draw the ledge you want to jump off.

Surely with all that practice shopping and thinking about shopping, women would be able to navigate the marketplace like a bloodhound, but that assumption has fooled me and many a man many a man-time.

Women don't know shit about shopping. They have no plan of attack and no philosophy. That's why whenever you go into a store with a woman to buy a crappy present for her best friend's wedding, you always end up in the purse section or the discount rack, even though it was decided to get her a set of wineglasses well beforehand.

Men do not shop. Even when we're shopping, that's not what we're doing. We do not wander aimlessly about waiting for some trinket to catch our fancy. Absolutely no fucking way. We're in, we're out, and everyone goes home happy, because they haven't wasted half of the goddamn day playing dress-up.

I feel bad for women sometimes. They can't even get good at the thing they love to do most: spending someone else's money.

PENISTORY 101: IF HISTORY IS A STAGE, WOMEN ARE THE GUM UNDER YOUR SEAT

History? More like penistory. That's what history should be called, since there's so many men doing so many fucking awesome things in it. Some people will tell you that women played a minor role in history. They're wrong. Women played no role in history.

Some woman in a documentary I was watching said women played a key role in the early domestication of dogs. I'm a man, so I enjoy documentaries, but I don't enjoy heaps of horseshit. Why a woman was in a documentary, I do not know.

"The early domestication of dogs required extreme empathy," said the wacky broad. "Thus, women did it."

That is a perfect example of what I call the Female Cycle of Dumbness. Women and their suppositions and cyclical logic are like fire hoses that no one's holding on to. No one's got any idea how it started, it's flapping all over the place, and if you stand there and try to deal with it, you're going to get a twenty-pound brass nozzle across your face.

One of the many things I've learned about women over the years is that there are a number of things they should never have on their own. I guess you could call it my Big Five of Man Things, That Should Be Completely Off-Limits To Women.

Dick's Big Five of Man Things, T.S.B.C.O.L.T.W.
1. Pink slips
2. Checking accounts
3. Screwdrivers
4. Opinions
5. Dogs

You know what role women played in the domestication of dogs? The part where someone bitches about how it shouldn't be done and that filthy animal needs to be thrown out of the cave. I can hear the shrillness echoing in my DNA.

WOMEN: NURTURERS OR TOTALLY IRRESPONSIBLE SADISTS?

Remember when you were in grade school and someone had to take the class guinea pig or sugar glider home over Christmas vacation? All the little girls raised their hands excitedly, and your male teacher hemmed and hawed and pretended he didn't see any of them until some boy raised his hand. Then the little boy took the guinea pig home for three weeks.

Your male teacher did that because a sobbing little girl dragging a dead guinea pig to class in a paper sack is a morbid way to start the school year.

Women can't take care of anything. Women can't take care of themselves, much less little animals or children.

If a woman's life isn't fodder for a weeklong series of talk shows and sappy mini-dramas by the time she's twenty-five, then it's a goddamn miracle, and she's probably hiding her relationship with a multiple felon somewhere. Either that or she was safely married off to a man by the time she was seventeen. Seventeen is when a woman is just starting to dip her big toe into the shallow end of disaster.

Hitler was raised by a single mother.

That proves men are better than women at raising children so fast that I need to take a breather.

Seventy percent of violent murderers and rapists were raised by single mothers.

That wasn't a breather at all!

If you think I'm lying about the facts, then you can get your big woman nose out of my book. Men only say things that are true—or at least things we think are true. We don't have time to waste conniving and sabotaging and looking things up when they're obviously probably true.

A child raised by a woman on her own is like a nonalcoholic beer you distilled by accident. Good work, you made a beer, but you left out some key ingredients like reason, personal responsibility, and the ability to not get your ass kicked every day for saying all kinds of fruity things.

PENISTORY 201: WHY WOMEN
CAN'T SHUT THE FUCK UP

Did you know the pubs of Britain close so early because of World War II? It's true. Pubs and bars were forced to close at eleven o'clock so munitions workers would be up bright and early for work the next morning. Men aren't fighters, we're lovers. We're lovers and we're drinkers—and we're also fighters. If you want us to fight instead of get drunk and bang waitresses, you're going to have to make a law about it.

Penistory also answers the age-old mystery of why women can't shut the fuck up for five seconds. Let's go back to the time of cavemen, when men carried sharp sticks and rocks instead of briefcases, and wore leather hammocks on their bananas and gave a fuck about nothing at all, and there was no goddamn divorce court.

Fuck, it was a good time to be a man!

Hunting is like fishing except that it is done on land. Or maybe hunting is like golf. Either way, the name of the game is shut the fuck up while someone else is doing it.

See that guy in the leather banana hammock over there who's about to take out a mastodon with his bare hands? Well, keep your fucking mouth shut about it, because we're hunting and a mastodon of that size will feed eighty women for a week. Keeping your mouth shut as a caveman meant being banana hammock–deep in starving women. You're thinking it's great, I'm thinking it's great, all the cavemen are thinking it's great, but everyone is also shutting the fuck up about it, because if they don't, a ten-ton fuzzy elephant is going to ruin everyone's shit.

Meat, women, and shutting the fuck up is in our MNA. That's man-DNA.

While men were out scrounging up the grub, women were at home doing nothing. Women haven't changed in a million years.

But Dick! Women did the gathering!

Women did no "gathering," men did. Men found some colorful fruits and vegetables on their way home, and after shitting the seeds on the ground outside their cave holes, men saw that the seeds grew into more fruits and vegetables. If anyone invented gathering, shitting did—not women.

How much work is it to walk outside and pick up a cucumber? If you don't know, ask the nearest single woman over forty.

Women chatter because while they were sitting around doing jack shit in the same place every day, they had to be as loud and obnoxious as possible to scare off predators.

Thanks, *penistory*, for coming to the rescue. The learning rescue.

A WOMAN'S SHELF LIFE IS NOT THIRTY

A lot of people will tell you women are no good after the age of thirty. It's called a woman's shelf life—the age at which

the benefits of starting a relationship with her no longer out-
weigh the staggering downsides. The second the clock strikes
twelve on that fateful birthday, a woman's face withers and
her hands turn into parchment. It's an ugly sight.

But it's also horseshit. A woman's shelf life isn't thirty. It's
twenty-three.

You can't fuck with women over twenty-three, and I'll
tell you why.

No woman under the age of twenty-three has ever
supported herself. She might have gotten a cute little job
running errands or selling clothes to other women under
twenty-three, but those aren't real jobs. Real jobs have titles
like Doctor.

At twenty-three, the real world lands on women like a
ton of bricks going about a million miles an hour. That's fine
for us men. We're made out of same mighty man-putty that
holds the universe together. We're flexible, pliant, our elastic-
ity is unlimited, and if you stick newspaper to our head, it
will leave a stretchy copy behind.

Women, however, are as stubborn and stupid as cement.
When real life comes tearing up the tracks of their twenty-
fourth birthday, full of swearing and guys in suits offering
them five hundred dollars for anal because they were in the
wrong place at the right time, it shatters their fragile woman
psyches.

Women over the age of twenty-three have their heads
screwed so fucking tight in the wrong direction and mis-
aligned that the threads are all fucked up. A woman did that

to my car's gas cap one time. How can you fuck up a gas cap?

That's why college is such a colossal waste of money for women. It's not like they need to learn anything, anyway. If women aren't married by the time they're twenty-three, they're never going to be. I don't have the statistics on hand, but I think a woman over the age of twenty-three has a better chance of being eaten by a bear than getting married to someone who isn't in prison.

Also, women don't need to go to college to meet guys. Frat parties don't ask hot women for their student IDs at the fucking door, do they?

No, they don't. If you've got a little girl, this book just saved you fifty grand.

FUCK THE PHONE

Men hate talking on the phone for the same reason lawyers don't use interpretive dance in the courtroom.

There are over five thousand muscles in your body at any given moment, which you already know because you're a man. I don't know how many you can control, but I would guess it is in the minority. I would guess 7 percent. That means there are 93 percent of 5,000 muscles in your body telling a story you're not meaning to tell. Some muscles are telling that story more than others.

That's a bit of subtle boner humor for you.

Women are simple creatures in heart and mind. They

like their stories simple, with shallow characters, and full of plot holes. For that reason, women can't appreciate *Patton* or The Three Stooges.

Women also like their communication to be as simple as possible.

When women are on the phone, you can't see their eyes glaze over when you mention the name of a great philosopher and how his thoughts so closely mirror your own. Women don't read philosophy. Don't be crazy. It would explode their heads and get glitter all over the furniture and fuck up your deposit.

Men need more out of our conversations. We need more out of life, too. To men, prattling away on the phone is like eating a baked potato out of a Dumpster with no butter or chives. It's like having sex with a woman who won't make you a bowl of cereal afterward.

Seriously, it's just a bowl of cereal. What the fuck? It's not that hard to get. It's not like you harvested the wheat.

PENISTORY 301: MEN ARE MAN-PRETTIER THAN WOMEN

Men are big and ugly while women are graceful, beautiful, and attractive.

This myth is so sneaky and seemingly harmless, I don't think there's a man on earth who hasn't said it without a second thought.

I don't know who the fuck started this myth; it was probably some seventeenth century mangina. And that just proves how awesomely powerful men are. Even the manginas can fabricate lies that last through the centuries.

Women are not better-looking than men. Women are not better or as good as men at anything. Watch me unfold this like a house of cards. You ladies out there who aren't allowed to be reading this and who are frothing at the mouth with anti-homosexual epithets for yours truly, be prepared to go fuck yourselves, because I took all the jokers out of the this deck.

Science

The male of every species on earth is the more attractive one, from insects to fish. Let's look at the male peacock, nature's pimp. He looks completely awesome! Female peacocks? Dumpy.

Penistory

I can count the number of classical works of beauty and antiquity that prominently feature women on my penis. One—the *Mona Lisa*. And everyone knows the *Mona Lisa* is not even considered that great of a painting; it's just famous because of *The Da Vinci Code*.

Michelangelo's *David*, Van Gogh's *Self Portrait in a Grey Hat*, da Vinci's *Man in the Circle Thing*—each one is an unforgettable masterpiece, and all are just like this book: men only. If women are so attractive, do you think they could at least make a cameo in the art history of an entire species?

Manclusion

The myth that women are prettier than men requires clar-
ification. It should not read "Men are big and ugly while
women are graceful, beautiful, and attractive," but should
instead say something like "Women will believe anything
they're told by a man who wants to fuck them."

WOMEN FEEL SORRY FOR LAMPS
AND OLD CHAIRS AND SHIT

Women are retarded when it comes to using their empathy.
Empathy is in your brain, not your heart or your stomach
as all women believe—and it's also in your balls; that's why
men are better than women at it.

Look around your man-self right now. Around you exists
a world of inanimate objects. What if someone came in and
took one of those objects away for repairs or something? As a
man you would think this was jolly good. Most things need
repairing, after all. It's good to know some man is doing it
and not some woman who would surely fuck it up.

A woman would be heartbroken.

"The poor item!" she would say. "He's being taken away
from all his item friends!"

I kid you not.

Let's say you accidentally knocked one of those precious
little bullshit items off of whatever it's on. You, as a man, would
be saddened that now someone has some extra work to do,

but otherwise the item could be easily replaced. A woman would be destroyed, just fucking destroyed. She would probably start an hour-long crying jag in the bathroom or take a sick day.

Women feel sorry for anything and everything. They feel sorry for sofas left out in the rain; they feel sorry for chairs with broken armrests that no one wants to sit on any more; they feel sorry for empty ice trays. None of it makes any sense, and none of it is interesting at all.

For women, throwing a penny off of a building to see if it will go through the sidewalk is the same as doing it with a kitten. They just can't draw the fucking line.

Women don't know anything about lines. Lines are hard and straight and get the job done. All women know about is curves. They need to stop overeating and go to the gym.

And for your *manformation*, a penny doesn't go through the sidewalk if you drop it off a building. That's a myth. A kitten might, though. I haven't read anything about that.

THERE'S NOTHING TO WRONG EXCEPT WRONG ITSELF

You hear this shrill, she-devil screech all the time:

Were you checking out that girl?

I carry around a special man-points medallion for any man to answer it correctly:

"Yep."

I was at the pub the other week, and the lady-bartender was wondering whether I should have another Seven and Seven. Lady-bartenders, who pour drinks like the liquor is free, are a pox on a moneymaking bar. Always go to female bartenders if you have the choice.

But a bartender's job is getting women as drunk as possible, not men, and definitely not me. Me is the last thing you want drunk in your bar.

Anything a woman says that ends in a question mark is her way of telling you she's the boss. Women don't give a shit about what you think or what you want. It's all them, them, them, and their no, no, no's. It's none of a bartender's fucking business how much I'm drinking or when I'm doing it, but the point is, women don't ask anything unless they want you to say "no," so always say "yes."

If for some reason you care to explain why you were checking out that girl, here are some reasons.

Men Notice Everything

Men notice everything, and we need details to grease the cogs of our massive man-brains so they keep spinning. Man-brains are like boats and motorcycles. If you let them sit, they need an expensive tune-up.

Maintenance is why we were checking out that girl.

Men Are Wary

Men are wary of all creatures that come within our personal

space. Our personal space includes (but is not limited to) our field of vision.

Your protection is why we were checking out that girl.

Tube Tops Are Fascinating. How Do They Stay Up Like That?
Physics is why we were checking out that girl.

On the other hand, if you're going to explain to a woman the motivations men subconsciously consider before everything we do, why not just explain democracy or gun control? Why not just sit a woman down and teach her why the men in her office are so eager to help her move? Women have the attention spans of children. Good fucking luck.

Women need a signal to know when they're supposed to get upset. If you act like you didn't do anything wrong, then you didn't. It's your goddamn right to check other women out.

Two hundred man-points!

ARE THOSE CATERPILLARS ON YOUR FACE OR CRAYON?

Women will do everything short of sewing a giant, red *A* for "Attention Whore" on the clothing of other women who get their breasts enhanced, but not one of them can stop fucking with her own eyebrows. How are eyebrow pluckings any different from boob jobs?

Answer: They're not hot as fuck.

Of all the stupid, time-wasting exercises women engage in for the sake of *Cosmetique*, eyebrow art is by far the stupidest and most time-wasting. Who are women gardening their eyebrows for, anyway? Men? Do any men subscribe to *Hot Eyebrows Monthly*? I've never even heard of that publication.

How about for other women? No, women don't look other women in the face. They just check out one another's bodies, so they have something cutting to say when they've walked out of earshot.

Women think the term "spare tire" is used only to describe other women's fat—they don't know that a spare tire is an actual thing!

Women must fuck with their eyebrows for caterpillars, then. They just want to make sure caterpillars don't try to have sex with their faces while they're sleeping.

BUT IT HAPPENED TO ME!

When I want an opinion on my broken car, I'll go to a mechanic. When I want an opinion on abortion, I'll go to a priest—not the single thirty-eight-year-old "party girl" across the street who needs pliers to zip her pants and a four-pack of Lynchburg Lemonades to unzip them.

Women can't get enough arguing. They love it because

arguing is one of the few things in life where fucking up at it gets you more.

Take pies as an example. If you go into a restaurant, dump a pie into your lap, and ask the waitress if she wants a piece, she's probably not going to serve you another one.

Arguing is not like pies. The less contructive listening you do, the further you get. For women, arguing is like a pint that's got a treasure map at the bottom that leads to another free pint with a map.

Of the many ways women like to argue, this is my least favorite:

You just don't understand, because it happened to me. And this is how I feel about it!

What am I supposed to do with that?

Women are the opposite of magicians. Whereas a magician will make an elephant disappear and then look like the most casual prick in the universe, a woman will do nothing and then look fucking astounded with herself.

If you want to see this dynamic in action, drop the "a" word around a group of women and see what happens. If you're in the right part of town, which is any part of town after 12:45 a.m. on a weekend, you can bet your ass half of them will say it "happened to them."

Somehow, letting a man pay for an abortion makes a woman an expert on the subject. That reminds me of the time I opened a dental practice after my parents paid for a cavity filling when I was eight years old. Or it least it would have, had I ever been retarded.

MOTHER'S DAY: BIG WHOOP

I forgot Mother's Day again this year, just like I do every year. You know what that makes me? Every mother's dream.

Mothers don't need a bunch of bullshit and spectacle for Mother's Day. They may want it, but for their own sake, give them nothing. A woman expecting a present is like a dog waiting for adoption at the pound. It's only going to be disappointed. Put it out of its misery.

Mother's Day was created by Hitler to encourage breeding among the Nazi nation. It was called *Muttertag*.

Muttertag was first declared official in Germany in 1933. Guess what was happening in Germany in 1933? A bunch of Nazi shit was happening. Nazi shit like *das Mutterkreuz*, a medal given to women who had cranked out more than eight babies.

Water also gives you life, but you don't take a day every year just to pay homage to water, do you? Where's National Air Day?

As I see it, I celebrated about 1,780 Mother's Days in advance from the ages of 0 to 5, when I had no choice in what unmanly things I was being dressed in and what unmanly things I was being made to do. I may have been forced to wear a *Guys and Dolls* sailor suit or sleep with a

stuffed pony—I don't remember the shit that happened
when I was six days old. But if it happened, I know exactly
who to blame.

Your mother already knows you love her. That's how a
vagina works. Once you've been in it, you don't have to do
any more work to show you care. That's also the foundation
of marriage.

YOGA IS FOR SLUTS

Yoga, pilates, power pilates, and aerobics all have one goal in
mind: to turn women into sex toys or sex pretzels, whichever
will land them a richer husband. Go look at some yoga pro-
motional materials at your gym and tell me there's one position those bendy little broads put themselves in that doesn't
hit your horny button.

Yoga has as much to do with health as health food: nothing.

Health food is just a way for women to define themselves without actually putting any work into it. As usual,
they spend someone else's money on the problem until a
philosophy patches itself together. Women doing yoga is like
dressing up as the Fonz for Halloween. You are not cool at
all, and you don't really ride a motorcycle. You just bought a
leather jacket.

Dick's Rule #1: Everything Women Do Is Meant to Attract Men
Women who are into yoga are just women who are really,

really focused on being sexy and want all men at the gym to know about it. They also want any men who get in their car to know about it. That's why they leave those stinking rubber mats in the backseat.

PENISTORY 401: DICK'S GREATEST WOMEN IN HISTORY

Grade school textbooks are great for drawing a flip book of a cowboy doing a cool little dance, but they're a shitty place to learn about great women in history. A much better place to learn about the great women in history is at a strip club.

All famous and historically significant women were either sluts or whores. If the facts say otherwise, keep digging until you find that I'm right. If you don't, you didn't dig far enough.

MARIE CURIE DESERVES A NOBEL PRIZE IN FULL OF SHIT

I'm so sick of all this Marie Curie nonsense. Every time a man makes a good point about how women couldn't do math even if it tasted like chocolate, some feminist or fifteen-year-old know-nothing drops this pile of shit in his lap:

"What about Marie Curie, you idiot!"

Marie Curie was not some super scientist who saved all women from the brink of total historical insignificance. Marie Curie, just like every other successful woman in history, was an opinionated, braying nag with a penchant for stealing the work of her diligent husband.

Marie Curie was the Courtney Love of the 1920s.

First, the very idea of women in chemistry is as funny as a fart machine.

Marie Curie didn't win any Nobel Prize, she won a *third* of a Nobel Prize. She had the support and *manssistance* of not only her husband, but also some other guy who probably wanted to fuck her. How typical of a woman to allow her business relationships to become inappropriately mingled with her personal life. If Marie Curie deserves any kind of Nobel Prize, it's one for cockteasing, which also shouldn't be rewarded, because it's not a great accomplishment. That's why there's no Nobel Prize for it.

I'm a man, so I enjoy history. Women loathe history as much as they hate being told they're just as obnoxious as their mothers, which they all are. Here's a lesson I've learned while reading books. Any time a woman is the first to do something, it's always complete bullshit. And I mean the kind of tangled nonsense you get when you duct tape a Speak & Spell to a mule and expect to have a smart-ass on your hands. It's a funny idea, but it's not really going to work.

Marie Curie was merely the first woman to be *allegedly* awarded the Nobel Prize. Just like Sandra Day O'Connor, Susan B. Anthony, Edith Wharton, Rebecca Felton, Lucy Stone, Madeleine Albright, and Sally Ride, Marie Curie is nothing more than an overcelebrated "runner-up" in the history of men.

JOAN OF ARC WAS TERMINALLY INSANE

There has been one and only one woman in the history of the whole fucking world who knew how to fight a cause for shit: Joan of Arc.

And Joan of Arc had syphilis.

And syphilis makes you crazy.

Saying Joan of Arc was heroic is like saying someone who's been drinking Jagermeister for three hours is fearless because he put his head through the windshield of a Peugot. He's not fearless. That's just what people do after three hours of drinking Jagermeister: put their heads through things.

FLORENCE NIGHTINGALE WAS A NEUROTIC PAIN IN THE ASS

Florence Nightingale was allegedly a large motivating force behind sanitization in hospitals and the entire profession of nursing, both of which have saved hundreds of man-lives.

However, Florence Nightingale doesn't deserve dick. She was just a neurotic clean freak like every other woman on the planet, and that's it. Do they give Orders of Merit for being a neurotic clean freak these days? Well, they did in 1907, when Florence Nightingale got hers.

Women may have possibly contributed in some piece-meal fashion to the practice of sanitization and the profession of nursing, but women have also destroyed millions of collective good times with their constant nagging about cleanliness.

Get your feet off this! Don't touch that! No more pudding in bed! Why is there a half-empty Jack and Soda in the shower?

Also, did you know obsessive cleaning might stunt the developing immune systems of small children? Florence Nightingale needs to own up to the blame for generation after generation of progressively sicker children.

Florence Nightingale is just a blind squirrel who found a nut-shaped rock in the dark. Time to sit back and wait for a woman to discover the cure for cancer through watching a twelve-hour *Sex and the City* marathon.

MOTHER TERESA, FUCK YOU

Mother Teresa never did anything other than con a bunch of nonprofit organizations out of free food and boarding. I have a cousin who does that. He sells computers that are about five years old and five times overpriced to child-service funds. He doesn't get any Nobel Prizes for that, though, and neither should Mother Teresa.

Like all the famous women in history, Mother Teresa was just the first one to do something. Bravo, Madam, you're the first woman ever to go help some children. That says more about women than it does about Mother Teresa. I was the first person to jerk off to Angelina Jolie in *Gone in Sixty Seconds*. I saw a special screening. I don't get a Nobel Prize for that, though, because I'm not a woman.

Mother Teresa was anti-abortion, claimed suffering was "a gift from God," her hospice workers were not protected adequately against diseases, and children were tied to their beds while millions of dollars in donations sat unused in banks around the world.

Saint Patrick killed all the snakes in Ireland. That's a miracle. Mother Theresa just showed up with a sob story and a quest to make miserable kids a hundred times more miserable.

MARGARET THATCHER IS A FIFTH-GRADE PIANO RECITAL

If women in history aren't famous for giving some famous or powerful man a blow job, then they're famous because they were the first woman to do something.

Even though I'm sure Margaret Thatcher has given her share of blow jobs, the reason she's famous is because she was the first female prime minister of England.

Big fucking deal. Men do the first of things all the time. What about the man who first got a snake drunk? I bet that would be hilarious, but I don't see his name anywhere in the history books. Men are all about quality and not quantity.

That's why we appreciate skinny women and not big, fat ones. And that's also why if Margaret Thatcher was a man, she would have merely an asterisk in the history books.

Margaret Thatcher didn't land on the moon. She didn't discover America. She didn't invent karate. All she did was show up for work and behave like a woman. How is that something to be proud of?

"I am the rebel head of an establishment government."
—Margaret Thatcher

Jesus Christ, this is the government we're talking about here. Decisions are made that send young, strapping men to their deaths thousands of miles away. Does self-promotional, narcissistic, female boasting protect against a mortar shell at two hundred yards?

Politics is a man's game. It takes finesse. It takes compromise. It takes the kind of patience men learn after a lifetime of dealing with women:

"The head of Jerkistan has a nuclear bomb you say? Well, that's not really a big deal. Just last night I talked a woman into shutting up for the best twelve minutes of her life. This guy won't be nearly as protective of his nuclear bombs as your average woman is about her precious fucking vagina. Vaginas are not made of porcelain—they don't break if you use them, for fuck's sake!"

GERMAINE GREER IS A CUNT

On September 4, 2006, Steve Irwin "The Crocodile Hunter" died off the coast of Queensland, Australia. Steve Irwin was one of the *mannest* man men to ever live, and his passing was as big a loss for the entire world as it was for just men. It was also a big loss for the last shreds of dignity held by the feminist movement.

On the day of Steve Irwin's death, Germaine Greer, a woman and a leader of the feminist movement—and allegedly a doctor, though of what I could not find out—went out of her way to attack the recently deceased Crocodile Hunter as publicly as possible and mock his untimely passing.

The points Greer wished to address in her article are irrelevant, just like everything feminists (and women in general) say, unless it starts with a "Do you think I should," or a "I'm so sorry I fucked up like you said I would."

A female marine biologist noted: *"It's really quite unusual for divers to be stung unless they are grappling with the animal and, knowing Steve Irwin, perhaps that may have been the case. . . ."*

"Not much sympathy there then." —*Germaine Greer*
Classy.

As she is a woman, I found it humorous that "Dr." Greer even uses the word "sympathy" as a part of her feminist vocabulary. Sympathy is something better people have. Feminists are the same creatures who routinely fabricate rape allegations in hopes of bringing down some mythical patriarchy one unlucky man at a time.

There's no such thing as a patriarchy. It's called the Real World, where seven billion strangers are picked to live in a loft and find out what happens when saber-toothed tigers start taking bites out of their asses while they're trying to sleep. In this Real World, men protect everyone, make all the right decisions, invent everything, and it's our fucking pleasure to do so.

"The only time Irwin ever seemed less than entirely lovable to his fans (as distinct from zoologists) was when he went into the Australia Zoo crocodile enclosure with his month-old baby son in one hand and a dead chicken in the other. For a second you didn't know which one he meant to feed to the crocodile."
—*Germaine Greer*

If you have any problem with Steve Irwin holding his infant son in his arms while feeding crocodiles, you are not only wrong, but you are also not a man—get out of my book.

Socially, we all accept a certain amount of risk and that stepping over the line incurs criticism. The question is, "How do we establish the risk of *X*?" If you have a vagina, no matter how empowered it is, the answer is always, "Well, how do I *feel* about *X*?"

Well, fuck you. The correct answer is, "Let's ask an expert."

Someone who built a multi-billion-fucking-dollar business on the dealings and doings of *X* qualifies as a bona fide expert. This expert dangling his own son over a bunch of *X*'s while doing *X* is a bona fide testament that *X* is not as risky as you fucking think, so long as you know what the fuck you're Xing.

Women never know what they're Xing. That's why feminism is fucked and backward. It puts a small amount of power in the hands of people who have no fucking idea what they're doing, ever: women.

All feminists are insensitive, horrid, and miserable; they have no families because they embarrass their parents until they're ostracized, and they alienate their friends until the only ones who remain are a small circle of self-loathing hags. Feminists have no children, because no man in his right mind would fuck one, and even if one was somehow drugged and tricked into it, Jesus would step in and perform the world's first immaculate abortion.

CHAPTER 4

Man Science

God and science have always agreed on one thing: Men are better than women. Where God left off by making it so, science picks up by explaining it. God, man, and science— all working together like a Swiss fucking watch. You can line up all the evidence like a row of beers and drink them down—like how women are shitty drivers and how Chris Farley was a million times funnier than Margaret Cho. You'd have a good-ass time, but it's not something you can put on your resumé.

That's where science comes in.

SPACE . . . THE MALE FRONTIER

If you're anything like me, you've never asked yourself why a woman has never been to the moon. The answer seems obvious: Women have never been to the moon, because the moon is chock-full of science. While this is absolutely true, it's only true in the way that there are no underwater unicorns. Yes, unicorns can't breathe water, but they also do not fucking exist. So what are we talking about?

The real reason women have never been to the moon has very little to do with their astounding ability to turn even the simplest of technologies into catastrophic disasters. For example, remember the last time you were enjoying *Die Hard 3, Payback,* or *The South Park Movie,* or any other time you were trying to mind your own fucking business? What happened? I'll tell you what happened. A woman ruined it with a torrent of shitty comments and naysaying:

"Nicolas Cage thinks he's so great."

"Those are fake."

"You only think you're funny."

"Cigarettes cause cancer."

Cigarettes cause cancer? No shit, I didn't know that. Guess what talking any more during *Face/Off* causes?

Can you imagine this manner of shit aboard the USS Scarface on its way to the moon? That's why women will never go there: their piss-poor attitudes.

OIL ON THE BRAIN

I read an article several months ago about some fundamental differences between the brains of men and women. I don't really remember where I read this article, but I'm sure it was in a reputable journal of scientific findings. If you happen to read about any of this somewhere, then that's where I saw it.

Because we men spent our time in science class listening and learning instead of giggling and passing notes about boys, I don't need to tell any of you how important the brain is. It's very important. It's more important for men, obviously, but the brain is still very important for women. I think it helps them keep their balance in heels.

Men's brain cells are coated in a kind of lubricating goo that conducts neurological impulses faster than those that are conducted in women's. Faster impulses mean faster thinking, which made a lot of sense to me in a hurry.

The very scientific article in my very scientific journal did plenty of pussyfooting around and bending over backward with crazy bullshit like "quick thinking does not mean better thinking," when in fact everyone knows it does. Regardless, the data were there in buckets to prove the obvious: Women's brains function about as well as a dry Slip 'n Slide.

That's how women's thought processes work—they run and jump and hit the rubber like a lawn dart.

Men have evolved into quick actors and quick doers with our mighty, lubricated man-brains. If you don't think lubrication is important, you're either a teenager or a woman.

A teenager because you don't know how to have sex, or a woman because of the same reason and you also don't know how to take care of a car.

ONE IN THREE WOMEN IS ILLITERATE

All men know we're better than women, because we live in the real world and we've kicked reality right in the ass while accepting women and their countless shortcomings. As men, what doesn't kill us makes us stronger. For women, what confuses the fuck out of them just makes them cuter.

Something like 30 percent of women are fucking illiterate. *Adorable.*

650 million women worldwide are illiterate. That's more than double the amount of illiterate men.

It sounds shocking, but when do women need to read? Reading is for knowing where the fuck you're going on the roads and knowing what the fuck you're doing when you're signing legal documents. Women don't do those things.

Numbers don't count as reading, so illiteracy doesn't impede women from writing rubber checks or measuring all the progress they're not making at the gym.

UNICEF and UNESCO say two out of every three illiterates are women. They put the worldwide female literacy rate in the sixties, while the male literacy rate towers above that at a manly ninety. I think you'll agree that that's plenty of numerical majesty to spare.

Initially, when I saw these figures, I thought to myself, "Maybe this is why women are so shitty at everything. Maybe women are just like that kid who is really bad at baseball, and then it turns out he just needed some glasses. Women just need to learn how to read."

Then I realized the so-called "writing on the wall" about every fuckup women step into is metaphorical. They don't need to be able to read to shut the hell up every once in a while and listen when someone other than Oprah dispenses advice about life.

WOMEN + MATH = DISASTER

Is there any science more manly than statistics? Fuck, maybe! But I don't care because after writing about statistics right now, I'm going to go eat a manwich and then throw a brick through a window. There's a 100 percent chance that I'll feel awesome about that.

Statistics is part of math, and math is for men. Do you know who agrees with that? Only the head of Harvard University.

Harvard has produced many great men of higher learning since it has been in business. They know who they are; I don't need to mention any of them here. Probably a bunch of presidents and whatnot.

The head of Harvard, which is a school most women would be lucky to marry a graduate of, said women suck at math and science. What he did was grant all women an honorary Ph.D. in in-your-face-onomics and declare math forever a man's game.

At the turn of the century, a mere 16 percent of engineering doctorates were awarded to women.

100 percent of those were given out of charity.

When it comes to math and science and using your brain, men have access to the cream of the crop. Our gray matter is top-shelf. We are driving high-performance thinking machines and moving mountains of ideas with our mighty man-brains, which operate like huge construction machinery.

Women, however, are using brains that resemble a broken tricycle one might find at a garage sale in the bad part of town. Women's brains reek of tetanus and squeak like a hamster wheel. Don't take it from me, though. Take it from a man who knows enough about math and statistics to make your fucking head explode. The former president of Harvard said something like, "Women couldn't do math even if it tasted like chocolate." Well, that's not exactly what he said, but we all know that women can't do math.

See what happens when women enter a field where good looks and cockteasing won't save your ass?

WOMEN HAVE COOTIES

Biologically speaking, men have more androgen in their systems than women. Androgen, as any biologist or man can tell you, is not only the key ingredient of awesome, but it also creates thicker, more resilient skin.

But androgen isn't the only reason why women's faces fall the fuck apart the second they hit thirty. It's also because twice every day of their lives, women plaster enough goo and junk on themselves to choke a donkey. Why do they do this, you ask? What am I, Mr. Answers with the answers to everything?

You bet your ass I am.

Do you remember the last time you went to bed with a woman without hearing either of the following:

"Don't touch my face. I just put some face softening and melting cream on it so it'll be fucked in ten years."

Or

"Hey, can you pass me the remote so I can get lotion and shit all over it that will never come off and will make your hand smell like vanilla every time you watch TV even after you've broken up with me because I'm a total bitch?"

No, you can't remember the last time you didn't hear any of that, and neither can I.

Women are embarrassed to be women. They wear masks every day of their lives, they wear clothing that says they're two sizes smaller than they actually are, and if they could get away with it, they would wear strap-ons and fake Groucho Marx mustaches and just call themselves men.

They couldn't get away with that, though. They'd have to trade their free SUVs for wedgies and kicks in the teeth.

WOMEN ARE ALL WHITE POWER

I'm not talking about racism, although women are racist as fuck. What's more manly than science? Nothing. Sports maybe, but otherwise nothing. And what's more science than the human brain? Also nothing.

In science, there's no room for emotion. That's not why women are lousy at science, though. Women are shit at science because they have the attention spans of little girls.

When did the myth even start that women act like bitches because they're "more emotional" than men? Does it not take emotion to die for your country and for freedom? Well, I think it fucking does. It takes a hell of a lot more emotion to fight for liberties than it takes to act like a cunt because someone forgot to pick up toilet paper at the store.

Women's brains are like men's brains, but without all the bits inside that makes them work properly. Bits like shutting up and *think-y before speak-y*. Those are all missing in a woman's brain, and in order to make up for these deficiencies, women have had to cobble together brains out of their existing, refurbished parts.

A study from the University of California, Irvine, says that men have 6.5 times the gray matter in their heads than women do, and that women have 10 times the amount of white matter than men do. Guess which matter matters?*

The gray matter, of course.

That's why your brain is referred to as "gray matter."

That's why a turkey sandwich is not called a "bread sand-wich." No one gives a fuck about the bread.

"Gray matter represents information-processing centers in the brain, and white matter represents the networking of these processing centers."—UCI, the university who sponsored the study.

In layman's terms, the study shows women are all bullshit and no bull.

Imagine a fire hose. As a man, that's very easy for you to do. Inside the heads of men, the hose works properly and puts out the fire. Inside the heads of women, they've got one end of the hose connected to the other. What the fuck is the point of that?

Women spend their entire lives mucking around in their white matter, networking bullshit that's got nothing to do with anything—and also complaining.

NEWS FLASH! MEN HAVE TESTICLES!

Men and women are perfectly equal, except for these things men have that make us jump out of bed at the crack of morning and ask what is going to get its ass kicked today no matter what happened the day before. Those things are called testicles.

Have you ever met an ugly woman who founded a suc-cessful company on her own? The only women who found successful companies are attractive as hell. They became "successful" women by getting handouts from successful men who needed some eye candy at the top. What the fuck are man millionaires supposed to do? Go to yacht clubs with a bunch of other dudes and millionaire sausage conferences? Don't be obtuse.

Successful men have failed many times in their man-rise to the top. It's called learning. You don't learn shit sitting around at home knitting, unless you are learning how to knit.

Successful women have never failed. All every successful woman ever had to do was show up in a low-cut top or give out a few unenthusiastic blow jobs. Either way, it doesn't change the fact no woman has ever done anything that involved risk in her life.

We all know it, and science even proved it.

A recent study says testosterone has a significant impact on the risks men are willing to retake for absolutely no reason. Absolutely no fucking reason, that is, save a big fat hash mark in the win column.

Well, no shit. I could have told you that without some government grant. Why else but because of testicles would men even talk to women or have sex with them at all, since women are so goddamn lousy at it? Another hash in the win column!

What scientists discovered was a marked rise in the testosterone of male subjects willing to play a worthless and meaningless game again after having been defeated. It is a simple step in logic to realize that this applies to anything and everything in life. Men don't give a shit about money or getting laid *per se*. That's not why we built spaceships and invented music and discovered the teachings of Jesus. We didn't do these things to get laid. We did these things because we have ants in our pants. Big ones!

Fuck biology and fuck science, since women can't understand them anyway. Men are better than women because when you shoot for a tie, you're the first loser. Men and women are equal? You just lost! See how that works? Come back when your balls drop—which will be never.

PAIN IN MY MAN ASS

Women only have one skill: the ability to have children. And it's not so much a skill as it is a defense mechanism against doing work. Kind of like how an octopus shoots ink all over the place when a shark is trying to bite it. Women crank out babies whenever a job is about to grab ahold of them.

Women also use the act of bearing a child as proof that they have a higher pain tolerance than we men do. Well, that's obviously some shit we've just stepped in. Now we just have to find the horse. Luckily, we're in the corral of science.

Dr. Roger Fillingim and some others conducted a study to determine which sex was more tolerant of pain and whether or not estrogen had any role in that. I don't really care if it does, because estrogen is gross, and I would appreciate it if women could keep all their hormones and juices to themselves. The study found that without a doubt, men can take more pain than women. Way the fuck more.

That's the most obvious thing in the fucking world. I figured that out the first time I was kicked in the bean machine and fell to the ground for several minutes. I had seen a woman do the same thing when she was struck in the head by a football. I would trade ten kicks in the head for one kick in the man-beans, and no jury of men in the world would convict me for that.

So where did this myth come from?

A woman would never pass up the opportunity to bray like a mule while being treated like a princess, so the myth didn't come from women faking stoicism.

Can you imagine a woman choosing to keep her mouth shut when she's just had a gold mine of attention fall on her? No, not even I can imagine that with my mighty *imangination*.

Women only appear to be more tolerant of pain, because they never do anything. Pain tolerance is like the Equal Rights Amendment. It sounds great on paper (except it actually doesn't), but as soon as women start having to live by it, everything falls the fuck apart.

Women never do anything until it's time to have a kid, and then they scream like holy hell and say that no man knows what real pain is.

I doubt childbirth even hurts very much at all. It can't

possibly be as painful as having to listen to the opinions of a woman all the time. That's a pain they won't even give you Demerol for.

TAKE TWO OF THESE AND CALL ME NEVER

Men are better than women at being sick. Men don't whine, complain, wear hideous sweatpants, or watch movies on the Oxygen Network all day. We don't crave anything, gain massive amounts of weight for three days, take mini-vacations while letting the house get dirty as fuck, go on crying jags, and we especially don't put moratoriums on oral sex.

How can you stop something you already don't do?

When women claim to be sick, they are faking it anyway. They get a sniffle, and it's SARS. They drop a teakettle on their pinkie toe, and it's broken. A woman sucks at reading, and all of the fucking sudden, she's got adult ADD or dyslexia. Nice bullshit, bullshitter.

Women fake everything, and now science can prove it.

Scientifically, women have better immune systems than men. Women don't even know what an immune system is, but theirs are better and there's tons of research that agrees with me.

But isn't that a good thing?

No.

Are you fucking serious? Does giving women charitable handouts in the workplace or in college make them any better at working or thinking? No. Does buying a woman a new luxury SUV because she got tired of her old one make her a better driver or not an ingrate? No, it doesn't.

WHERE'S WALDO'S Y CHROMOSOME?

People who know nothing about science (women) say that the Y chromosome is slowly vanishing from the human species of earth.

That means in a billion years, there won't be any more men. There also won't be any more functional machines, libraries, people to type women's school papers for them, or anyone around to explain what the fuck happened. What a woman paradise that would be. No machines to get anything done, no learning or reading, no religion that makes any sense, no explanations for fucking anything. No responsibility and no causality.

Too bad that Y-chromosome disappearance is a bunch of shit.

Women are all like Hitler—they talk a big game about a lot of idealistic shit, and then the first thing they pull out of the bag is genocide and mass extinction. Here's an example of something a man might say, followed by a woman's response:

"Due to lack of stress from not being the sole breadwinner of the family unit, women outlive their spouses and collect government pension funds for years to come while not contributing and never having contributed a goddamn thing. Women are

therefore leeches on not only the economy, but the very principle of economy."

Now here's a typical woman's response:

"If it weren't for women, you wouldn't even be here, you gay bitch! You woman! When your Y chromosome disappears, you'll all be sorry for not treating us like the one-hundred-sixty-pound princesses we are!"

Touché, madam. And congratulations.

The reason the Y chromosome isn't going anywhere is because it's God's chromosome. It has all kinds of secret abilities and all this other mumbo jumbo I don't even want to get into, because we're here to talk about why men are better than women and not a bunch of fucking science. If you want to know the details, get a degree or just open your mouth. You're a man; the right explanation is going to come out no matter what you don't know.

What male scientists found was that the Y chromosome has an extra brain gene. It's one of four Y-chromosome components, or gears or whatever they are, that throw four switches in a fetus from girl to boy. While no one knows what this fourth brain gene does exactly, I'm going to take a stab at what it does:

It turns the brain from OFF to ON.

SPELLING, AND ALSO CHLAMYDIA

For men, something like herpes spells death for a thriving sex life. It spells it with the letters: S-T-D.

Guess what venereal disease spells for women? G-O, go. As in go party, go hook up with a bunch of guys, and especially go have as much promiscuous fun as you want. The world is your sex oyster.

Fifty percent of sexually active women have had chlamydia in their lives. That's absolutely true, just like everything I have ever said. It's also fucking staggering! It means the woman you're about to have sex with has a chance of being lousy with venereal disease governed by a coin toss.

Heads or tails, you're fucked! How many men bring condoms out to the club every weekend, even though there's way less than a 50 percent chance they're getting laid? A lot. Most, in fact. That's the difference between men and women. Men play the numbers and play it safe, especially when our dicks are on the line. Women just wander through life with their fingers crossed and their eyes shut, thinking that as long as they can't see the chlamydia, the chlamydia can't see them.

FEELINGS KILL

Feelings are the source of all womankind's greatest fuckups and inadequacies and also the reason women hate children so much.

Feelings not only ruin all sexual encounters, but they also inhibit the healing process.

A new study from the University of Missouri-Columbia says manly men heal faster. Men were given surveys and then measured on their recuperative progress. The ones who showed a marked restriction in their emotions while answering the survey healed about a million times faster.

I'm not talking about shit Neosporin will take out in a few days either. These men suffered brain damage and spinal cord injuries. Emotionless men's brains and spines healed faster than those of women; probably because women are emotional train wrecks and feelings fuck you all up.

Penn & Teller

On an episode of their cable TV show, *Bullshit!*, Penn & Teller encouraged a group of subjects to openly release their emotions and a control group to behave sensibly. Guess what they fucking concluded? The expression of feelings results in the exaggeration and amplification of these feelings. Men have known this all along. Emotions are a bullshit contest that women sign up for at the age of two and participate in their whole lives. No wonder women haven't accomplished shit. They're training for a fucktathalon of emotions every waking minute of every day. I would be exhausted too, except that I'm a man and I am never tired or sick.

MEN HAVE BOUNCERER BRAINS

I've gone on record saying women have the memories of goldfish. A goldfish is a creature that will eat itself to death because it has forgotten gorging itself not five minutes before.

Saying women have the memories of goldfish, however, isn't true. Women remember shitloads of things. They don't remember anything worth a damn, like directions, or to bring a fun attitude to bed with them instead of their mother's, or that work doesn't start at 9:35, it fucking starts at 9:00.

A recent study says the ability to think critically, aka take care of business and get the job done, is not a function of memory, but of selective memory. "That is fucking interesting," I thought to myself selectively.

Let's say that thinking critically is like flushing a toilet. You have your problem floating in the bowl and the solution comes about when you yank on the handle. A bunch of swirly shit happens, and then the problem is gone.

That's how a man's brain works: problem, flush, solved.

A woman's brain is exactly like the above except that no one has flushed in years. As any man will tell you, a toilet chock-full of anything, especially shit, is not going to flush. What it is going to do is make one hell of a huge, horrible mess, which only makes this metaphor ten times more true and hilarious, because that's exactly what happens when women think.

"Until now, it's been assumed that people with high-capacity visual working memory had greater storage, but actually it's about the bouncer—a neural mechanism that controls what information gets into awareness." —Edward Vogel, a man

If brains were nightclubs, man-brains would have huge burly dudes out front who look like that guy Zeus in the movie *No Holds Barred* with Hulk Hogan. That was a good movie. They don't take any mumble-mouths, and if you're dressed like a slob, you don't get in. Anniversary? How about a punch in the face? Happy anniversary.

Women have a sign out in front of their nightclubs with a bowl of candy that says "Please only take one candy." Some asshole did that in my neighborhood every Halloween, and all the candy was always gone after two kids. Or maybe he just put out an empty bowl and a sign. That would have been smart.

Women pack their brains so full of shit that "get your oil changed" and "don't act like a bitch" get shoved out the fire escape to make room for "Ryan at work likes motocross" and "love means never having to say diet."

Women have no concept of priority in memory, just like they have no concept of priority in life. If you've ever seen a woman try to balance a cup of hot coffee and a baby on top of her car while pumping gas, then you know exactly what I'm talking about.

THE ANSWER IS: TELEVISION, SYPHILIS, AND CATS

Like every man in the world, I fucking hate cats.

Women can't get enough of cats though. Apparently

women also can't get enough of having their brains eaten by parasites. Guess what that explains?

A lot.

Toxoplasma gondii is a damn brain parasite found in cats' intestines. I haven't read very much about it because this book isn't about a bunch of boring medical bullshit, and it definitely isn't about cats. When it's on *House, M.D.*, I'll learn about it, but not a second before.

As far as I'm concerned, having a house that reeks of cat piss and shit is worse than any low-grade brain parasites anyway. Both are permanent conditions and a miserable way to live your life.

But I did read enough about *Toxoplasma gondii* to see the words "cats" and "severe brain damage." Holy plausible theory, Batman! It's another drop in the Grand Canyon-size bucket of why men are better than women.

Women love cats like they love high heels and abusive boyfriends. They just can't get enough of anything that will leave them damaged. Clearly, that extends to their brains. I looked up some brain-damage symptoms, in order to prove my suspicions.

"Symptoms of brain damage include: eating too much or too little . . ."

If I could summarize all women in one sentence, that would be it. It's like innie/outie belly-button classifications, except for the entire species of women. Either she's a too-muchy or a too-littley—most likely the former, but praise Jesus if it's the latter, because you've got a real nutcase on your hands who's good for about four months of yuks.

"*. . . Agitation, lethargy, or irritability. Feelings of worthlessness, hopelessness, or inappropriate guilt.*"

These symptoms proved to me that *all* women have fucking brain damage, not just the cat owners.

"*Toxoplasma gondii can be transferred to the host by cleaning a cat's litter box, or touching anything that has come into contact with cat feces.*"

That's pretty much everything in a cat-woman's house, including her pillow. If you ever enter one—which you shouldn't—but if you do, just throw your jacket in the mud outside or in the middle of the street. There is no chance in hell you're not bringing it out of that house as used kitty toilet paper.

"*Possible symptoms include: muscle aches and pains that last for a month or more . . .*"

In the end, I couldn't find a single symptom of brain damage that all women didn't have. That brings up the age-old question: How can you tell if a useless pile of shit is broken? It's a useless pile of shit, so what the hell is it supposed to do?

Children know a lot about a lot of things. They have an innocent wisdom that is revered in spiritual texts throughout humanity; boys do, anyway. In this case I think we can learn something from the boys:

Women have cooties, brain-eating cooties.

THE PROOF IS IN THE PENGUINS

Once upon a time there was a shitload of penguins that lived in Antarctica. One day every year, all the penguins got together and had sex with each other. Eggs were laid, and if you've ever had a kid, you know what happens next. The women assume they are done, fuck off completely, go and eat until they are so bloated on fish carcasses they can barely walk. Needless to say, their big fat demeanors have not improved.

The plot I'm describing is the force behind a brilliant documentary about penguins called *March of the Penguins*. It was made by men. Unlike women, men need to achieve things in order to be famous. We need to climb impossible mountains and brave harsh Antarctic conditions to make brilliant documentaries. Men have also wrecked Ferrari Enzos on the Pacific Coast Highway while completely hammered, which is incredible.

Penguins can teach us a lot about surviving in the cold and catching fish, but they can also teach us a more important lesson about men being better than women. In *March of the Penguins*, the females are completely fucking useless. They only go like a month without food while the males go four; they are conveniently gone during the monthlong portion of the mating season that involves wedging an egg the size of a softball in your ass and balancing on your goofy-looking feet against two-million-mile-an-hour winds; and they are constantly making noise.

The only thing the penguin women did right is square

off with one another during the mating dance. I don't know exactly how much man has in common genetically with his penguin ancestors, but I don't think you can have a penis and not enjoy a good catfight.

The women penguins also can't protect their baby penguins for shit—just like regular women. When they come back from their sea banquet, sliding on distended, fish-packed bellies, and send the males limping toward the leftovers at one-third a healthy penguin weight, some of the first shots we see are of local hawks just swooping down casually and picking penguin babies off like bread crumbs.

Frankly, it made me sick, and I don't know how you can watch that scene and not think of every single child who's ever been abducted in a playground while an irresponsible mother sat twenty feet away yapping incessantly on a cell phone and sucking down a four-dollar coffee.

Women also perpetrate just as many child abductions as they cause through negligence. Guess what we see in *March of the Penguins?* When one of the new mothers, fat on fish jelly, accidentally drops her baby to a death on the freezing tundra, her first move is to swipe the baby of another.

Real classy, ladies.

WOMEN: ARE THEY SMARTER THAN HORSES?

Every day and thousands of times a day, women go back to abusive spouses or hit REPLY TO ALL on an office e-mail even though the buttons are clearly labeled and that is obviously not the right button to press to just reply to one person. It's a sex e-mail we're talking about, for Christ's sake. It says "cock" like seventy times. You don't think the filters are going to catch that? How about take an extra two fucking seconds to make sure before clicking the worst button on earth?

In a new study, doctors Paul Irwing and Richard Lynn say men are smarter than women. But a study without statistics is like a strip club with nipple pasties. It's not really a strip club, is it? It's an indoor beach:

Women are, on average, five IQ points stupider than men.

Twice as many men than women have an IQ of over 125.

A Genius (an IQ of 155+) is 85 percent more likely to be a man.

Women have pockets on jeans that are too tight to put anything in.

Women are also bad drivers, get pregnant at the drop of a dime without a job, and have never ever completed a crossword puzzle without the help of a man.

FEMALE MOSQUITOES AND FEMALE WOMEN ARE THE SAME

Did you know only female mosquitoes suck your blood? That's right. *Mansquitoes* don't do shit but relax at home, I guess; whatever a mosquito would do if it weren't being an asshole.

Women and mosquitoes both:

1. Suck your blood
2. Never stop buzzing in your ear

Gender is transcendental. Women mosquitoes suck blood; human women suck your life and your dreams right out of your head. Man essence is easier and more fun to get at somewhere else, but women don't go down for either easy or fun—just for money. Otherwise, everything has got to be the hard way all the damn time, like watching a broken *Rudy* DVD that skips and stalls before anything pays off. It's just a bunch of work.

THE SIGNS OF DUMBNESS

Astrology is one of the dumbest and most worthless things in the world.

Astrology is so dumb, I don't think even a man could come up with something dumber. That's because ten thousand years ago, or whenever it was that astrology was crapped out, a man sat down and said, "What's the dumbest thing that I could possibly crap out? Astrology!"

Even though men invented it as a joke, we are still better than women at astrology.

Generally, men avoid the whole mess completely and file all that pathetic bullshit in a huge plastic bin that says Someone Else's Problem; like how men deal with menopause. Fuck it.

Men don't give two shits about astrology. Sure, I can tell you which signs are the water signs and that the month you were born in means you like bologna sandwiches more than a kick in the face, but I can also tell you that Bennie and the Jets wore electric boots and mohair suits.

Astrology is all a bunch of meaningless crap that bored men made up with their infinitely powered *imanginations* thousands of years ago. That's one point for men for wasting time on purpose and no points for women. But then why am I able to tell you things like a Leo can eat half of its weight in chocolate and Scorpios are laziest on Tuesdays?

I'll tell you why. For every lame astrological fiction I have in my head, women have a hundred. For every insipid and vague prognosticatory paragraph that I've read by accident, women have read a thousand on purpose. They live and breathe horseshit. Women have the whole astrological *shitiverse* memorized; every page, part, and parcel of puerile nonsense. Women are so fucking desperate to define themselves with something that's not their long list of fuckups and failures, they cling to astrology like the anchor of a sinking ship.

Women don't look for answers, ever. They only look for instructions and excuses, for which astrology is perfect.

This is your character, this is what you're afraid of, this is why you don't have to feel bad for acting like a bitch all the time: You're a Taurus. And if you ever do feel feel bad, you just have to open up the daily paper to see if today's a day you *should* be feeling bad.

Try it out for yourself. Learn a little astrology as a lark, and see if it makes talking to women easy. It's like learning magic tricks to shut small children the fuck up: It works.

THE PREGNANT BRAIN

Women's brains are like a urinal on a boat: useless. At least that's what I always thought. A recent slurry of scientific data, however, says women and their silly baby-making actually fires up their dormant brains. What they use them for, no one can guess—unless someone was going to guess "goldbricking."

Pregnancy increases the size of certain neuron areas in women's brains.

In other words, pregnancy makes a woman's brain bigger and more manlike, and thus better.

Using the brain to rear a child stimulates brain growth.

How about that? Using the brain, something a man does every day while amusing his friends and coworkers and while keeping the entire fucking world from careening off into hell, makes the brain better. The brain is like a coupon. You leave it sitting on the counter for a month while you refill your coffee and chat with friends on the computer all day, and when you try to use it at Shifty Joe's Fish Shack, it's not worth a goddamn thing.

Virgin female rats took five times longer than mother rats to find hidden food.

I've never known a virgin who could do anything worth a damn, let alone find free food. Isn't free food why women invented "not being a virgin" in the first place?

I guess now we know what postpartum depression really is. It's the devastating aftereffects of nature removing a woman's mental blindfold and forcing her to see the world through manlier eyes for the very first time. That's why pregnant women turn into emotional disasters. It would be like a man waking up and realizing he'd been wrong about everything.

WOMEN ARE AS COLD AS AN ICE-COLD BEER

Women are constantly cold, and they constantly cannot shut the fuck up about it.

Allegedly, women feel colder than men because they have a higher surface-to-volume ratio and less muscle density. That's a nice way of saying women have a higher body-fat percentage than men. And that's a nice way of saying women are fat as houses.

The huge muscles of men are like little nuclear reactors, built to simultaneously power and warm our tremendous minds. Unlike the minds of women, men's actually work. That's why we need more warmth. When you prove something to a woman, you need to do it with crayons on construction paper. If you can't, then you're speaking Greek to her. And if she is Greek, then you're speaking Pig Latin. And if she's a pig, why are you even talking to her?

Being naturally skinny is just one more wondrous thing men are better than women at. That's why Curves, the women's gym, is taking off like a shithouse fire.

Actually, Curves is successful because it's run by a man. If Curves were a gym for women, run by women, it would be about as successful as "lesbians" raising a child. Welcome, kid, to Ass-Kick City. Population: you.

Women are colder than men because they're fat and love to complain. If you need anything more scientific, why the fuck do you think they have periods—for fun?

THE SUBCONSCIOUS MAN-BRAIN

Science should be renamed "man's best friend." Or better yet, if science could combine itself with a dog, then we'd be talking.

We would not be talking about those Sony Aibos either. Those things are pieces of crap.

Actually, fuck dogs. Ever since dogs allowed themselves to be put in purses without biting the fuck out of everyone, science has taken over their spot. Better luck next time, dogs.

A new study says the unconscious brain is a better decision-maker than the conscious variety.

"*. . . too much thinking about it led people to make the wrong choice. Whereas, if their conscious mind was fully occupied on solving puzzles, their unconscious could freely consider all the information and they reached better decisions.*"
—*Ap Dijksterhuis, a man*

That explains why men are so much better than women at not fucking up their lives so bad the government needs to set up temporary housing for them and their beaten children, just so they can hope to get a waitressing job. Big fucking accomplishment. You can get pregnant, but can you refill my coffee more than once?

If thinking were baking a delicious meat pie, women would upend a bag of fast food and Cool Ranch Doritos into a casserole dish and then drop it on the table with a frown and a diatribe about how you're about to not appreciate something worthless. We men slow-cook our ideas on the mental back burners where the think-grease has been collecting in the brain pan for decades. That's how you get the good flavor. It's that old grease in the back.

Men let their *submanconscious* do all the thinking. Think about it. Or better yet, don't! As a man, you'll reach the correct decision either way.

WOMEN: HOMEWRECKERS FROM BIRTH

The worldwide divorce rate is like 50 percent. And if it isn't, who cares? The point is, in addition to being loudmouthed and lazy, today's modern woman doesn't know how to compensate for her shortcomings in marriage by shelling out some respect.

These days, women have opinions instead of chores.

Women are always the reason for a divorce: your wife, her bitchy friends, her mother, even your own daughter, all conspire against you to fuck up something that's sacred. Women are sacrilegious as shit.

Don't believe me? Perhaps you'll believe my friend, Science.

Gordon Dahl and Enrico Moretti are responsible for the following data:

Parents of girls are 5 percent more likely to divorce.

Parents of three girls are 10 percent more likely to divorce.

Single mothers of girls are completely fucked. Women are poison to a relationship, no matter what their age. Whether they're making ten cents on the dollar neglecting their children at some stupid Barbie Dream Job, or just being ten and playing with their Barbie Dream House, women ruin marriages.

When I found out about this study, I was appalled. Little girls are even smaller and more helpless than women. Girls know even less than women and need at least as much assurance and assistance as their larger and more opinionated counterparts. But what if all that extra attention ruins a marriage?

Little Girls Cost Way More to Raise Than Little Boys

Men have something called *imanginations*. We can turn a cardboard box into a spaceship or a race car or an outhouse at a construction site. Little boys don't need constant babysitting and they don't need a bunch of expensive clothing and shiny bullshit. Little boys can read books.

But nickel-and-dime shit aside, today's modern little girl needs to have both her wedding *and* college financed! That's the double dip that broke the marriage camel's back.

Little Boys Wig the Fuck Out in Divorces

Boys incentivize a happy marriage. Do you really want your bedroom furniture burned or to drive your teenage son every day, because he's banned from the school bus? No way!

No One Wants a Daughter

It sounds harsh, and that's why women are banned from reading this book, but while everyone loves their daughters, not one of them wanted one. Cindy Crawford loves her mole, and Owen Wilson probably loves his penis nose, but at some point, both were massive disappointments. A son might start the next IBM or join the Marines. That's something to be proud of.

What's a daughter going to do? Marry rich?

Just like keeping a full-size woman around, having a baby girl involves a lot of charity. Take a lesson from China: Have a boy instead.

WOMEN FEEL SORRY FOR RAPISTS

Women involved in any level of government other than typing up the spun gold that comes out of men's mouths or making the coffee is a blueprint for disaster. Not a disaster like being two hours late to a party because your wife can't read directions, but burning sulfur raining out of the sky and lava shooting all the fuck over the place in a biblical manner.

Women feel sorry for themselves too much to get anything done. It's all the fucking time with them. They can't even have fun when they're somewhere phenomenally fun like a Nicolas Cage movie or at the beach getting taught how to throw a Frisbee correctly, because they're too busy feeling sorry for themselves.

Boo-hoo, you have boobs—you were born with a AmEx Black Card. Get over it.

Women feel sorry for you, too. Even if you were filthy rich and for some reason you could fly, every single woman out there would still feel sorry for you and also hate the fuck out of you somehow.

Women feel sorry for puppies and kittens and little baby seals with their priceless little hides and their cold little flippers. They feel sorry for diet sodas and imitation Oreo cookies. "Does anyone really love diet sodas for diet sodas?" women ask. "Do they love diet soda because of its taste, or in spite of it?"

Women feel sorry for worn out T-shirts and washing

machines. They feel sorry for broken-down cars that get traded in and old pairs of scissors that get lent and then are never seen again. They feel sorry for rocks and sticks and smudges on tissues and broken glasses and doorknobs that rattle and flat tires on the side of the road. Women wallow in sorrow every day of their lives like their parents left them in the inflatable kiddie pool and then went on vacation without them.

Women even feel sorry for rapists.

A recent study has concluded the following:

When people who deserve it get what's coming to them, men's brains function as men's brains do: 100 percent perfectly. Women's brains, however, are donkey shit.

Women's brains lit up with empathy like slot machines when a deserving party was administered a mild electric shock. Men's brains lit up with glee. By extension, we can assume women have zero concept of justice.

Women are coddling know-nothings who can stop a buck about as well as they can hold on to one.

An eye for an eye is coded in men's *MNA*. We can thank God for putting it there. You remember God, right? He's the guy who gave you a dick.

SO WHAT'S THE DEAL WITH TRANSSEXUALS?

When it comes to the topic of men being better than women, where the fuck are transsexuals?

Just like it has an answer for everything, science has an answer for this: Men are better than women at being transsexuals and also at being gay. It's the same thing anyway, probably. What the fuck do I know?

Here's an interesting set of scientific man-facts that prove my point. Proving points is what makes science so manly. And then gloating about it afterward with even more science, that's so many man-points you'll need a man-bag to carry them all to the man-bank.

A study from the University of East London determined that gay men use their brains like women, but also like men. Sex with women may not be a gay's cup of tea, but using their brains for more than a pillow weight is.

"Gay men adopt male and female strategies. Therefore their brains are a sexual mosaic," says a doctor involved in the study. "As we expected, straight men used more compass directions than gay men or women, and used distances as well . . . but gay men recalled more landmarks than straight men, as well as using typically male orientation strategies."

If you didn't follow all that or skipped it because it was boring, let me sum it up: Men are better than women at directions, and we're better than women at life. What's more important in life than knowing where the fuck you are? You can probably think of something, but that's only because you're a man.

When giving directions, women use landmarks like "Turn left where my husband yelled at me last week" and "Remember that coffee commercial in the eighties with those four women reminiscing about a ski trip?"

That's real useful on the road.

A friend of mine has a favorite saying: "You can't polish a turd." I don't know where he learned it, probably from another man. That's how wisdom is passed down through the ages after all, and also why we have rocket ships and penicillin instead of donkey carts and syphilis. Women keep any wisdom they manage to scrape together locked up like it's their PIN number.

If you think female-to-male transsexuals are men, I've got a brand new Ferrari to sell you. I painted it on the side of a sack of shit.

CHAPTER 5

The MANifesto

Truly, is there anything greater and more manly than being a man? Absolutely not. Sometimes I wish I was a woman so I could appreciate how wonderful and *mantacular* we men are without the spoiler of my all-knowing frame of reference.

But then I wouldn't be a man. And that's no life for me, Dick Masterson.

The following MANifesto is all the manly things that there could possibly be and all the manliest ways in which men are better than women. You won't find any science in these parts, my friend. This section is packed full of something more logical than science could ever be: manliness.

WEDDINGS ARE GOLD TOILETS. FLUSH.

Is it any surprise that a woman's second favorite pasttime—having a wedding—is a huge waste of time and money?

It sure is.

Weddings are a complete waste of time and money and are the stupidest thing that a new couple or anyone can do.

Here's a hypothetical situation that may or may not have happened six thousand, five hundred times a day every day this year in America alone.

Johnny Everyman (twenty-five years old with a degree in business and economics and a summer job selling kitchen knives) is going to enter into a bond of legal matrimony with Jill Princess-Complex (twenty-two with a degree in art history who has never had a real job in her life). Sound familiar? You bet it does.

Is this new couple going to:

A) Put a down payment on a house with their savings and monetary gifts from family members and friends?

B) Elope for like a hundred bucks to beautiful and romantic Downtown Courthouse?

C) Have an *extravaganzic* gala that will drain their bank accounts, stock their kitchen with glitzy, overpriced wares from Eddie Bauer that they will never use even once, and condemn every moment in their relationship from that point on to sulking in the shadows of anticlimactic disappointment?

Men know weddings are stupid, because men are better

than women at starting a family and at laying the foundations of a healthy relationship with a significant other. Call us wusses if you want, but it's completely true.

Even on women's home turf—weddings and engagements—men can run circles around them. For instance, how many women know the Six *C*s of diamonds, the main components of any engagement ring? As a man, I can just rattle them off the top of my head. And for all you know, I'm not even married.

The Six *C*s of diamonds are:

cut
clarity
color
certification
carat

And of course the sixth *C* is the one wearing it.

Calling a comb "indestructible" doesn't make it so. It's still just a plastic piece of shit. A dream wedding is equally delusional.

WHAT ARE MAN-POINTS?

Good question. Let me award you your first man-point for asking. Let me then tell you that I'm sorry, but answering that question would be a severe loss of my man-points.

Here's a few other examples of how man-points can be gained or lost. Usually listing them is a loss of man-points, but since I said I'm going to do it first, it's a huge gain of man-points. Man-points are like that. Sometimes you don't know you've got them until they're gone, and sometimes you don't know they're coming until you're up to your ass in them. You can figure it out from there. That's the fun in life. That's why men don't read manuals and why women only read books about rich sluts whoring it up.

Dick's Ways to Get Man-Points
Catching a drink that has fallen off the table
Disregarding directions
Using the phrase, "I think I know what I'm doing."
Not wearing a jacket
Being sneaky for no reason
Throwing a sandwich in the street

Dick's Ways to Lose Man-Points
Talking about man-points
Lighting a cigarette on the wrong end
Turning the cigarette around and smoking it anyway
Locking someone else's keys in their car
Keeping track of man-points
Using the phrase, "I wasn't crying."
Calling your girlfriend or wife

At any time, man-points may be retroactively gained or lost and may be done so with a multiplicative modifier, depending on the circumstances. Here's an example.

Dick's Example of That
Dancing.
Definite loss of man-points.

Riverdancing, on a table.
Negotiable gain of man-points.

Spilling a woman's drink while Riverdancing on a table.
Loss of man-points with a multiplier.

Offering to hold the woman's spilled-on belongings in your man-bag—and she's also drunk and has a huge rack.
Congratulations, you just won all the man-points.

Holding an ugly woman's belongings in your man-bag.
Loss of all man-points.

Man-points are one of my favorite *mantivities,* and as men I'm sure you'll enjoy them. If you're new to man-points, just remember what I always say: Try not to get your nuts kicked.

WOMEN TRADED IN COOKING AND CLEANING FOR BLOW JOBS

Ever wonder why the only place you can get a fresh-baked apple pie these days is at Marie Callender's or your grandmother's house? It's because during a movement called "Women's Liberation," women traded in cooking and cleaning for blow jobs.

It's just like when men traded in working for listening to women's endless screed of woman problems. Except that never happened.

Men don't operate like that. We don't trade shit we don't want to do for things that are easier.

Responsibilities are not baseball cards. They can't be traded or sold to the highest blow job. Responsibilities are more like tattoos you've gotten when you're drunk or depressed. They may not be the prettiest things in the world, and they may not make any sense, but goddammit they're here now. Someone's got to deal with this shit.

Imagine if men worked like women. When we invented farming and agriculture, we would have just stopped hunting altogether and became a vegan species. Then all of our hair would have fallen out and our asses would have gotten flabby as fuck, because vegans are disgusting and lack so many vitamins and nutrients they're hardly even human.

Would you like some fries with your Big Mac? No, because there's no such thing as a Big Mac in a world where men acted like women. There's no meat at all, just a bunch of aimless dreams and junior high grab-ass.

PETS ARE NOT CHILDREN

Talk to any woman about anything, and eventually she'll tell you exactly the same thing:

Men are dogs.

Just like any other time a woman opens her mouth, she doesn't have any clue what she's talking about. She's right only this time because a woman spews words from her mouth with such frequency and ferocity that eventually she has to be right, even though she's likely contradicting something she's just said or possibly jibbering in a language she doesn't know.

Dogs are loyal, resourceful, and, most importantly, they have positive attitudes. What could be more manlike than that? They also don't give a shit about being too clean, because that is neurotic and it fucking ruins the feel of a home.

Those are man-traits, and men share them with all the other animals in the wild that have to make their own way instead of goldbricking on the couch day in and day out.

How many times have I seen a dog in a sweater or a purse? Not a lot, but when I have, a man wasn't perpetrating it. A man has also never had a bunch of pictures of his pets in his wallet, ready to whip it out on the unsuspecting at a moment's notice like a creepy guy in a trench coat at the park. A man will also never tell stories about his pets until someone throws up out of boredom. I have seriously done that.

No one gives a shit if the hamster likes raisins more than

sunflower seeds. Fluffy is scared of the vacuum cleaner? I would be pretty nervous too if some massive machine came roaring recklessly around my neighborhood—that's why I'm nervous around women in SUVs.

Pets are not babies. No matter how much a woman wants you to think the pug in her lap has been growing inside of her for nine months, it hasn't. It was a few hundred bucks, and there's like a billion of them. No one wants to see pictures of the ugly thing, no one wants to hear about its first poop, and no agency is going to come if the fucker misses a few meals or gets the shit slapped out of it. It's not a big deal.

Taking care of babies and pets and classic cars comes naturally to us men. It's our sixth sense. It's our man-sense and mighty *manpathy*. The only thing women can empathize with is a cactus. Women should be so lucky as to be cacti. Then no one would ever want to have sex with them, and their problems would be fucking solved.

WOMEN WOULD VOTE FOR HITLER

A woman voting for anything other than *American Idol* or her favorite type of chocolate is like watching a small child run full speed into a wall. The child runs. He's going somewhere at full speed, and there's no doubt about that. But very quickly, you realize that the fundamental understanding of the process as a whole has been perverted.

Then comes the wall. Then comes the crying.

Women would vote for Hitler, not only because a woman can be talked into buying a ketchup popsicle while she's wearing white gloves and it's currently raining free ketchup popsicles, but because women are all fascists. I've had more than a thousand women tell me I deserve to have my dick cut off. Why do women think it's so fucking funny to talk about men getting their penises cut off? It's not funny at all.

But let's leave the constant threat of castration out of it for the moment.

Anyone who's married will tell you a lot of things. The first is: "Don't get fucking married for any reason, you dumb shit." And the second is: "Marriage is not a democracy."

Marriage is a fascist dictatorship of oppression, as is any relationship with a woman. Work relationships, professional relationships, "professional" relationships, they're all the same. If you don't like the flavor of the Kool-Aid and you want to add some mix, prepare for an assault. They enforce their opinions through the constant threat of violence, and if it escalates from a wailing siren of bullshit in your ear, it will be because women are always the first to hit during any kind of dispute. It's not even a percentage. It's as much of a guarantee as it is that the sun will rise tomorrow. Women hit first 100 percent of the time. There was another person who pulled those shenanigans: Hitler.

As men, we understand the sun rises because it's actually a star that our planet rotates around. It's actually we who are spinning around the sun, and therefore it's guaranteed to rise. Women don't even fucking know that!

Every morning when a woman wakes up at the crack of 10:30, she's thrilled to shit to see that the sun's in the sky once again and that her fake tan will look just as radiantly orange as it did yesterday. That's one of the biggest reasons why women shouldn't vote. They don't know anything about planets, suns, or how not to look like an Oompa Loompa. Also because, if given the chance, all women would check the box marked "Savagely Beat or Kill Anyone Who Doesn't Agree with Me." That will always hold women back more than any mythical glass ceiling.

THE CAR SAYS, "VROOM!"

Women love purses and shoes and all kinds of glittery shit, because it gets them attention. Don't let any woman tell you she's not into jewelry, purses that little dogs can fit into, and that kind of crap—all women love it.

There isn't a single woman alive who can resist the charm of a cheap-looking handbag made by orphans in another part of the world, who are whipped and starved half to death while they slave over a pair of pink flip-flops decorated with little snowmen wearing sunglasses.

That's how easy it is to make a hot women's fashion item. I just did it right there. Just think of the stupidest thing you can think of: How about flip-flops with snowmen wearing sunglasses? And look at that, I just shit myself because that's the cutest goddamn thing on the beach. A stupid snowman wearing stupid sunglasses.

How about a cat with a little pilot's hat flying a biplane? Also, his name is Top Kitty!

I just made myself sick.

Women are as predictable as falling off a ladder you've got stacked on top of another ladder. And here's some more advice for you young men: Those kinds of cutesy bullshit things are not signs that a woman is fun, easygoing, or interested in snowmen or anything else for that matter. These little markers are signs of the *opposite*.

Men are better than women like sports and cars and sportscars are better than purses, shoes, lip gloss, cheap jewelry, and anything else made by whipped Asian kids. No matter how much you whip the shit out of some orphan, he's not going to know how to assemble an AMG Roadster.

THERE ARE NO GOOD WAYS TO SKIN A BEARD

Shaving is one of the manliest things there is—and so is not shaving. The definition of manliness is having the ability to do something, but then choosing either to or not to do it.

Thousands of years ago, men evolved beyond pissing on things to demonstrate ownership. Women, however, have not. Women piss all over you by turning your face into their own personal Wooly Willy.

It looks sloppy!

Women don't care at all how a beard looks. They don't care about how anything looks besides themselves.

It scratches my face!

That doesn't even make sense. If a beard was scratchy, then it would scratch the face of the man wearing it, as well. Unless we are to believe that men are somehow magically immune to getting scratched by our own beards, or that beards are the one-way mirrors of itchiness?

MAN'S REAL BEST FRIEND: BEER

Have you ever made beer?

Probably.

Your answer is "probably," because that's a manly way to answer any question. As a man, I don't really care what your answer is anyway, because I already have a point to make. Like any man, I'm taking responsibility. Women only ask questions to land you in a heap of shit.

"Is that you standing there?"

"Probably. Why are you asking?"

Because why the fuck *would* she be asking?

Ambiguity is good *manjo.* Here's my next question: Have you ever thought about making beer?

Probably.

At least once in his life, every man has looked down at a glass or a bucket of tasty brew and thought to himself, *Where does this come from?* Just like a woman asks when she looks at her thighs after the age of twenty-four. Gross.

Beer is a man's true best friend and his only lifelong companion. Dogs, man's former best friend, don't live long enough to be a lifelong companion and, even worse, they attract women.

That's why men invented beer. The powers that be didn't provide a suitable companion for man on the entire earth, so instead of bitching about it, man devised his own. Beer is a counterpart to man birthed in his own glorious image, in that it gives constantly and consistently without ever asking for recompense. Beer is man's gift to himself.

Beer makes all jokes funny. Beer makes ugly and fat women attractive, which is something ugly women can't do for themselves, because they're too busy getting fat. Beer is also refreshing and a good listener.

Men make beer and men drink beer for reasons so pure and manly that they make me want to stop writing immediately and go chop down a tree with an axe while telling my wife or girlfriend that I'm not dancing tonight or ever.

What's the analogue of beer for women?

Women must have something that sums them up in the same way that men have beer. They'd like to say it's a beautiful flower or better yet a porcelain vase, but I've never seen a porcelain vase in the shape of a bowling ball, and I don't think lettuce is a flower.

I WANT TO BE A CRACK WHORE WHEN I GROW UP!

Men are the super adhesive man-glue that holds society together by the seat of its ass, and women are that crappy sticky strip that holds Post-It notes on your computer screen. Women don't stick to anything, and goddamn it if you ever get that strip of gummy residue off your monitor. Thank God someone reminded you about Carol's stupid surprise birthday cake in the conference room in five minutes. Now you get to remember it forever.

Remember back when you were twenty-five and you thought of how much better you could make the world if you were Batman or Hugh Hefner? How about Steve McQueen or James Bond or Indiana Jones? My point is, the heroes and role models of men are our springboards to success. Role models are the whip master of the conscience and a lifelong commitment to toeing the line. Men and young men have always looked to the heroes of history and cinema and thought to themselves, "Boy, I sure want to emulate that guy and thereby increase the global quality of life." And it works.

Now, try to think of a female role model. Give it some real man-thought. Sigourney Weaver from *Alien*? Yeah, that's about all I could come up with too. And as we all know, that part was written by a man for a man. Imagine how much better that movie would have been if it had actually been played by a man. I bet some chick's top would have come off.

Here are some alarming answers I received from women of all ages when I asked them to participate in the very same thought experiment:

Paris Hilton

Tara Reid

Princess Di

Their mother

Promiscuous sex and drunken debauchery? Women set the bar so low they'd have to dig a grave just to fail.

MEN, THE SAFE-SEX SEX

I was reading an interesting book called *Freakonomics*. I'm a man, so I try to read as much as one book per week. Women do something similar, except instead of *Macbeth* it's *McCall's* and instead of Sartre it's *Seventeen*.

The book *Freakonomics* posed an interesting theory that crime took a downfall in the nineties because of legalized abortions fifteen years earlier. That got my man-juices turning and my man-cogs churning.

Unwanted babies cause crime? Unwanted babies are probably unplanned babies, and unplanned babies come from unprotected sex. Now whose fault is it when people are having unprotected sex?

Women. Unprotected sex is 100 percent women's fault.

There is no reason that it should even be possible to have unprotected sex in our day and age. The odds of having an unplanned baby should be one in a billion. Every child born that isn't planned should be the next Jesus Christ. The last time I checked, a billion to one covers the court's definition of *immaculate*.

The only reason any fetus is ever aborted is because of a woman. Some woman was too lazy or too stupid to put on a raincoat when it was raining men. Women also can't take their birth control pills for shit. Sometimes they take them in the morning, sometimes they take them at the gym, sometimes they take three at a time so they can go relax for a weekend at Lake Havasu without a bunch of bother.

If the police find a meth lab in your house, guess who goes to prison? If Chevron finds oil under your house, guess who gets a big fat check? If someone finds a delicious ham in your oven, guess who gets the praise?

You do. You go to prison, you get the check, and you get a honey-glazed pat on the back. But if it's a woman's house and a woman's oven and someone finds a big unwanted bun in it, somehow in the world of women and their crappy magic math, it's 50 percent your fault.

That's absurd.

Women are to blame for every unwanted baby and every abortion in the world for the same reason everyone laughs at you when you're hung over. You knew exactly what would happen after drinking thirty pints, you dumb shit. You did it anyway. You get heaps of man-points, but you can't trade man-points for sympathy at the prize arcade.

Have any opinion on abortion you want. You're a man,

and that's your right as a man. What can't be argued, however, is that every abortion and every unwanted pregnancy is
a woman's fault.

To every man who's ever paid for an abortion, completely masculine kudos to you. You're more responsible than
the would-be mother you bailed out, and you're a thousand
times more generous than Mother Teresa. Women are first in
line to claim ownership of their bodies, but once the debts
start stacking up, they're willing to sell some stock.

WOMEN ARE THE SPECIAL OLYMPICS

If there's one thing you learn after dealing with the mentally
handicapped, it's that they all want to be treated equally.

Also: graham crackers.

Women are a lot like the mentally handicapped in that
way. The only difference is women don't deserve equality or
graham crackers.

History is filled with examples of disabled men overcom-
ing obstacles and taking care of business in a manly fashion.
Several presidents have been handicapped. Also that guy
from *Goonies*, I'm pretty sure he was retarded.

No matter how many chromosomes a man is born with,
he wants the playing field even. He also wants to be treated
the same as everyone else.

What a fucking surprise that a woman invented the
Special Olympics.

The Special Olympics is for the mentally handicapped what a Chinese lady with an umbrella is for me. It's something that I do not want around. Chinese ladies will stab your goddamn eyeballs out with those things.

One time, I was watching the Special Olympics and I saw a retarded weight lifter throw up about two gallons of orange juice. It was so hilarious that a decade later I still think about that image at least once a week. Does that sound like the kind of thing the mentally handicapped need?

No! It's humiliating. The mentally handicapped need training for minimum-wage jobs and volunteers to help them keep their shit together. They don't need committees planning fucking parades and testing them for steroids just so they can go out and throw up a cubic foot of orange juice on national television. You can't not laugh at that no matter who you are. Jesus would have laughed at that. He probably would have pissed himself.

When a woman hits the gym for two weeks in a row, she needs parade floats to honor her fat ass. That's why women have such a hard-on for the Special Olympics. They think accomplishments aren't accomplishments until they're shoved down everyone's fucking throat.

I respect the shit out of retarded athletes, but that's where it ends. I don't print the sentiment on a bumper sticker and then use it to devalue the chrome backside of a fifty-thousand-dollar SUV some man paid for. That would make me a woman instead of a different gender which brims with class and discretion.

The Special Olympics is the only organization legally allowed to use "Olympics" in its title. It's just like how women are the only other species legally allowed to use "man" in their name. Except for manatees.

A SCORCHING CASE OF BULLSHIT

Winter is the season for some of man's favorite things: tight sweaters for women, and fire. I was starting a fire last night when the following occurred to me:

I have never seen a woman start a fire. I don't think a woman ever has.

The only thing I've ever seen women do while a fire was being started was bitching, and I'm not so sure they knew a fire was being started at all. Women don't understand cause and effect in the same way we men do. That's why instead of saying "Let's go eat," they say "I'm hungry." Instead of saying "Can you turn up the heat?" women say "I'm cold."

Women have no concept of power or self-determination. That's why they whine about what they want instead of just getting off their ass and putting on a sweater or eating a sandwich. That'll be how the first female presidential campaign sinks to the bottom of the ocean.

"But Madam Senator, have you ever started a fire?"
"No. My husband takes care of that."
Damn right he does.

IGNORANCE IS NOT CUTE

Dating is similar to interviewing for a job. At least for men it is. Men tout themselves and list their accomplishments; often we have to do so several times, because women get distracted by things like neon signs and words they can't pronounce.

Men list what we have to offer with a smile, and then we allow a respectable time for the other party to reach a decision or a blow job.

A woman, whether on a date or a job interview, will just try to look cute or slutty, depending on how old she is. I really couldn't tell you which way it goes as she gets older either, more cute or more slut. Women are like roller coasters: slut and cute just go up and down randomly with age. The only thing you can count on is the big terrifying drop at the end.

Women think the best way to attract men is to act dumber than shit. I know I've said a lot about how dumb women are in this book. They're certainly dumber than men, and maybe they're even dumber than a dead horse. No dead horse has ever driven my car to the store with the parking brake on. No dead horse ever shaved his eyebrows and then drew them back with a pencil.

In spite of all that, women are not nearly as stupid as they act.

Every woman on the whole goddamn earth thinks ignorance is cute, but it isn't. Hang around some women sometime and see for yourself. When they get together, it's like they're having a Stupid-Off:

"You don't understand computers!? Wait till you hear what I don't understand! I don't understand toilets! Or rain! I don't understand rain! Is it angels crying, or what? Does it come from the ocean? There are dolphins in the ocean!"

Congratulations. You're so cute, you're functionally retarded.

Women have "playing the part of a helpless dimwit" permanently ingrained in their collective heads like an Etch-a-Sketch that's been left out in the sun. The only thing you can do is cross your fingers and hope the last thing you sketched wasn't a dick or else Mom's going to be pretty pissed off for no real reason.

MOMMY DEAREST

There's a special person in every man's life he learns to appreciate the day he moves out of his boyhood home. This is someone who should be respected at all times. This is a person whose grace knows no bounds, whose advice is spun with golden threads of experience and tempered with kindness. This person should be treasured, and above all else, this is someone to whom a man can confide all of his deepest secrets.

It's his attorney. Who did you think I was going to say?

Women all listen to their mothers. That's why their lives

are all about a Cheerio away from total calamity, and they never know what the fuck they're doing. A woman getting the advice of her mother is like a kid who needs glasses getting two kaleidoscopes . . . and then being shoved into traffic. Good luck, four-eyes!

No man on earth listens to his mother. He listens, technically, but it's like how a man listens to a crappy fifth-grade piano recital. It's an exercise in tolerance and a nice thing to do.

When women listen to what their mothers are saying, they're actually *listening* to the fucked-up advice. Then, even worse, they're thinking about the fucked-up advice, and then ultimately they manage to fuck up the fucked-up advice in a way that somehow makes it more fucked-up instead of less— they fuck up *fucking up* the fuckup. That's women. Fucking up the unfuckupable since the Garden of Eden.

THE INSTITUTION OF MARRIAGE

Think about this next time you're going to get married: Your woman would have married a rapist or a murderer just as eagerly as she's marrying you.

Women love attention almost as much as they love money. To them, money and attention are the same thing. Women are simple like that. Usually the things they like are actually the same thing. And you can trade both money and attention for sex. Women love stalkers, babies, and black eyes. They're all just heaps more attention.

Have you ever seen a group of women at a wedding having a Cry-Off? That's the game women play when they see who can get the most emotional over stupid crap. It doesn't matter who wins. What's important is who loses, and that's you.

What's the worst thing a man's ever done? I don't even care and it doesn't matter, because nothing could be dumber and more transparent than marrying a convicted murderer. It happens so often that the news doesn't even report it anymore. It's the invisible menace that is women and their attention-mongering.

If the media was run by men, which it should be—and which it also is, but I mean more obviously, like how a man runs a dogsled team—then women and their gratuitous fuckups would be on a permanent ticker-tape parade across the bottom of the screen.

"*. . . Local woman trades child for new Xbox video game console . . . Fat woman surprised when heel breaks . . .*"

That's what you'd see on CNN. There would also be more swearing on the news because men don't have sticks up our asses about saying "fuck." That's a waste of time and a misuse of asses.

Why would a woman marry a convicted murderer? Does she have unresolved issues from her childhood? Yeah, that's probably it. Or at least it would be it if this were a new-age fantasy camp for hugging and playing bongos and patting yourself on the ass for doing nothing. It's not. This is a book about men being better than women.

A woman marrying a murderer is like a man marrying a woman who has a neurotic compulsion to make sandwiches and a twin sister who gets really drunk all the time. Anyone on death row has shitloads of attention at their disposal. They have so much, it overflows their glass daily. And then it's just surplus, begging to spill all over an eager would-be prison-bride.

There's also no potential for sexual contact in a prison marriage, so it's every woman's fucking dream come true.

FEAR: MAN'S COMPASS

Women have no fear of anything.

They have no fear of any shit breaking, because some man will always fix it in an attempt to fuck them—which always works. They have no fear of regrets, because they have no memory. They have no fear of losing their jobs, because they don't ever really support themselves anyway.

Women especially have no fear of saying or doing anything stupid.

Fear is a manly thing. Without fear, a man wouldn't get the Popeye adrenaline he needs to accomplish heroic man-feats of car lifting and lion fighting and tearing trees out by their roots. Does Red Bull do that for you? I don't fucking think so. Without fear, a man wouldn't think to himself, *Maybe I shouldn't get herpes from this drunk skank.*

Fear is a man's life compass.

The fear of looking like a jackass, the fear of getting kicked in the teeth for "accidentally" grabbing some seemingly unattended woman's boob; fear is what keeps men coloring within the lines and preparing for rough weather ahead.

Women fear nothing.

Women are like the eight-year-old who wins the spelling bee for correctly spelling "establishment." We're all very impressed, kid, but you'll still feel like a jackass if I pour this punch all over the front of your pants like you pissed yourself.

That's life, best to shut your fucking mouth.

THREE TIMES A WHORE

Did you know you're liable for child support if you knock up some slut who lies about being on the Pill and then doesn't want to have an abortion because of some ridiculous shit like she suddenly has "principles" or because her mother didn't abort her? You are liable, and it's the biggest crock of shit and injustice that could ever be imagined.

Look, where were all these magic, money-sucking principles while you were on your back enjoying the greatest four and a half minutes of your life? If someone offers you a Snickers bar and you don't want it, and then that person wins a plasma TV or some jet skis in the contest on the wrapper, you're not entitled to shit.

If men have absolutely no choice in deciding whether a fetus is unconceived or given up for adoption after birth, then they have no legal responsibility to pay for the goddamn thing. Is this Law for the Retarded 101? This is how the court proceedings should go:

"Have you motherfuckers ever heard of No Taxation Without Representation!?"

No, I'm joking. You can't say "motherfuckers" in court.

"Your honor, if you go rent a car and opt not to tell them you're blind, you can't just drop off the car later with a new sun roof, two missing wheels, and Delorean-style doors. It's not their problem, it's your problem. Case closed."

If you take money for something, then you took money for something. Sometimes that makes you a professional lawyer and sometimes it makes you a professional doctor, and when women accept alimony or support for a child the father didn't want to keep, it makes them professional fuckers.

Isn't there a word for that?

WHEN WOMEN SHOULD SHUT THE FUCK UP

I hear this question all the time:

"Dick, you're such an expert on women. Tell me, what qualifies a woman as a perfect wife?"

I have only ever heard this question from men, because women don't give a fuck about what makes a perfect wife. All women care about is being the perfect soccer coach: crappy snacks, endless drills, and no sex.

The perfect wife is one who knows when to shut the fuck up. Indiana Jones said it best:

"You're insulting them and you're embarrassing me."
—*Indiana Jones*

When Women Should Shut the Fuck Up
1. When a man is talking or might start talking
2. When a man stops talking
3. When in doubt
4. When not in doubt

Imagine you're at a cricket match. You don't know how the game works, because no one does, but you know when to cheer and when to leave, because everyone else is doing it. That's how men do everything in life. If someone else is doing it, we do it. Like war, which is awesome.

To women, the whole world is as confusing as cricket. But instead of just going along with it when everyone starts clapping, they run out on the field and start telling the players they're doing it all wrong.

IT'S ALL DOWNHILL FROM HERE

It's part of your man-nature to go through a midlife crisis. A man gets old, he gets bald, and he gets comfortable in his job and his marriage. The only thing that will cure his ailments is a brand-new convertible.

Notice how I didn't say "an affair." That's how women go through their midlife crises. Men buy a cool new toy to tool around town in and blow through yellow lights at sixty-five miles an hour, and women destroy families.

The average age of a midlife crisis for men is forty-six. That's right at the point where a man realizes the big drop in the roller coaster of life was at the beginning, and no one told him to stick his hands in the air. Oh well. It's nothing an enormous TV or a skydiving ten-trip pass won't solve, at least until he herniates his back on the second jump.

The average age of a woman's midlife crisis is seventeen. At that point, women get a glazed look over their eyes and start talking about ridiculous things like goals and dreams and soul mates and a bunch of other bullshit they have no intention of doing. Men rattle that shit off during their midlife crises too:

"I'm going to be a painter."

But a man only says it once. Then the crisis is over. With women, it's wave after wave of silliness in the wavepool of delusion that is their lives:

I want to be a lawyer!

I want to be a CSI!

I believe in animal rights!

Sure you do, honey—maybe we should give them the right to vote!

For us men, a midlife crisis is a time to reflect on and

manpreciate the things we've accomplished. We might have a family, a great career, or a hilarious neighbor friend with a funny catchphrase. The only thing women realize during their midlife crises is that they've never fucked a black guy.

THE SAVING GRACE

Throughout the ages, men have become timeless legends for sharing their unique gifts with the world. Mozart was a famous music man. Hippocrates was a famous doctor man. Richard Simmons was a famous girlie man. Need I go on?

Aside from Amelia Earhart and Dolly Parton, women have only become famous for one thing: sucking cock.

Monica Lewinsky, Cleopatra, Mary Magdalene, who can think of any women more legendary than those harlots? Joan of Arc doesn't count, because she was a schizophrenic. These days, we lock your ass up for that.

Men can be painters or baseball players or even chefs. Some men have been so creative that they thought of the Smurfs. *Manpressive.* Also, men share our talents with the world. The only thing women share is how much they want everything you have.

Women have natural talents too, I guess. I mentioned the large breasts already. Unless you think Dolly Parton is famous for singing. If you think that, then you've obviously never heard of Dolly Parton. Women can be talented, but if you try to appreciate them for their talents, they'll call you a shallow jerk.

Does anyone think Liszt went to his grave bitching and moaning about how everyone loved him as a composer and a musician, but they didn't love the *real* him? What the fuck does that even mean? And Mozart never broke up with someone for bragging about his operas. That's childish.

Men know that we are nothing more than the sum of our parts. You are your talents, your job, and your car; so all three of them had better be awesome. If you build bridges, don't act surprised when they put "bridge builder" on your tombstone. That's what you fucking were.

On the other hand, there's an old joke that says if you build a thousand bridges and suck one cock, you'll be remembered as a cocksucker. Sorry, ladies, it doesn't work in reverse.

ALL WOMEN HATE GUNS

Guns are awesome. In fact, a gun is the manliest thing there is. Guns are like a penis that makes things blow up.

Fuck!

I take that back. The manliest thing there is would be some kind of nuclear car with guns attached to it. But is the car manlier because of the guns, or are the guns manlier because of the car? What about a tank? Where does a tank play into this?

Wherever it wants. It's a tank.

All men love guns and think guns are the greatest thing that has ever happened. Did you know that without guns 99 percent of people on earth would be slaves? Guns ended slavery.

Before the invention of the gun, mankind lived in a feudal society. I have seen the film *Braveheart* many times, and each time I watch it, I become more and more certain that feudal life was bullshit. Guns invented democracy.

As a man, I thank guns for that. If I were a woman, I would have to figure out some way to have lackluster sex with the invention of the gun. That's how women show gratitude. Women hate loud things like fun parties and football games, because no one can hear their inane and catty comments. Women also might hate guns because they're complicated—guns, not women. Women are not complicated at all. Women are as simple as broken vending machines that eat your money.

Guns are complicated as shit. They have moving parts and require care-taking. I heard a female comedian say vaginas are complicated. I doubt that very much, but that's what she said. I could hear her crystal clear, because no one was laughing.

The real reason women hate guns is because women enjoy being in danger. Without guns you, me, and everyone would be on constant alert for the Hun Alarm that would jolt us out of bed in the middle of the night and let us know our town was about to get burned to the fucking ground . . . again.

Thank guns and all the men in the military that you've never heard of the Hun Alarm.

THE MIRACLE CURE FOR ED

I heard about something called ED last night. Apparently ED stands for erectile dysfunction and it's a problem for some percentage of men. If you have ED, there's a 100 percent chance you also have SW, because SW stands for shitty wife.

If your house falls apart because the builder forgot to put nails in, whose fault is that? If you don't know, there's a lawyer somewhere willing to help you figure it out. If you go to a work-related picnic and you remembered to bring the cups, but everyone else forgot to bring all the food, whose fault is that? It's not yours. Thanks to you, people don't have to drink out of their hands like monkeys, even if they are still going to be hungry as fuck.

ED is entirely the fault of women. Here, I'll prove it. Find me one happily married man with performance problems.

That was a trick question. There has never been a happily married man.

Dick's Miracle Cure for Erectile Dysfunction

Cheat on your wife.

If something inside your man-gut tells you that's wrong, it's merely your mighty man-conscious trying to fix something that's broken in the world by fixing it in you. Men lead by example. And we set examples with our balls. Have you ever heard of Gandhi? No woman even understands what he did.

The truth is, there's no such thing as cheating. It's not a vice. It's a perfectly natural thing. Cheating is Father Nature's way of telling us we have a debilitating case of SW. Cheating is the miracle cure for erectile dysfunction. I put a thirty-day guarantee on that motherfucker.

SHITTING IS AWESOME

There are two things in life you can count on: death and shitting.

Fuck taxes, women invented them.

Sometimes I listen to the conversations of women. Sometimes like when two women going in two opposite ways are stopped in the middle of the fucking street just because they saw each other driving. You're driving, I'm driving, let's throw a fucking parade about it.

All women talk about when they're on their own is men, and who can blame them?

Men are dirty!

False. Men are spick-and-span. Ever heard of Mr. Clean? There's no Miss Clean. There is a Mrs. Butterworth, though. A fat, sticky cow.

Men have no feelings!

I guess some woman directed *Schindler's List* then.

All men talk about is the toilet!

Half true.

Men specifically love talking about the big number two: Captain Deuce; the high-flying cargo drop; Steamboat Charlie. So what? Pooping is the first thing human beings learn how to do. You, me, the pope; everyone still has to take a shit way before they get their hands on any Bibles or typewriters or whatever it is that you do. And once men master something, goddammit we stick to it. We never stop enjoying it. For men, the destination is the journey, and the toilet is an inspiring metaphor for life.

Men are going to keep talking about shitting long after we learn how to do it. We're going to keep perfecting it and ourselves by bringing it to the forefront of conversation and discussing it openly and honestly—and hilariously. That's manly.

NOW YOU'RE TALKING DOUBLE-TEAM

My best ideas come to me while I'm sitting in my second-favorite chair drinking Black Label. *Polygamy is the only way to go*, I thought.

Let's explore that.

"It takes a village to keep a husband." —Hillary Rodham Clinton

I'm not sure if Hillary ever said that, but she should have. Women aren't up to the threefold tasks of pleasing a man. Those tasks are: intellectually stimulating a man, sating a man's voracious sexual nature, and giving a man the precious emotional support that he doesn't need at all and which I totally just said as a joke.

Women can't do any of those things. Just look at the smartest woman on earth. What's her name? That girl with the advice column. Dear Abby? She's supposedly a "genius" and her column is so boring that I've never even read it.

In the world of women and their lame problems, it takes the smartest woman out there to tell you your husband is cheating on you and that your son is gay—or vice versa. Get a fucking clue, ladies. The smartest man in the world is curing cancer and inventing the Internet.

Sexually pleasing a man is a two-woman job, minimum. The last time you were having sex, who were you thinking about? See? Two women. You were practically having a threesome right there, and that's worth six thousand damn manpoints.

As far as I'm concerned, bigamy is the only way to go. It may be "illegal" and "frowned upon," but the men of the past found ways around these so called "laws." It's time we turn back the clocks: the sex clocks.

THE UBERMENSCH

Superman is to Men as Lois Lane is to Women.

If you said that to a woman, I bet she would actually feel good about herself.

But she should feel like shit.

If a man is so inclined, he can learn everything he needs to know from one source: Superman. How to act, how to treat the less fortunate, how to live lies and lead a double life; it's all there for us men. That's because while Superman may be an alien from another planet, he's still a man.

Any man has the same chance of being a flying, cape-wearing alien with the ability to spin the world in reverse to undo an earthquake as any woman has of being a competent, confident career woman.

Lois Lane is a successful woman just like like Superman is a man who can jump over skyscrapers and stop trains. A woman has as much place in the byline of a major news publication as a man has in a pair of tights fighting robot monsters in space. That's how absurd it is.

And that's not even mentioning that Lois Lane is an attention whore and a single-minded maniac who constantly sticks her nose where it doesn't belong and usually ends up costing Superman huge chunks of time to pull her ass out of the fire and her head out of her ass. In that amount of time, thousands of people die in catastrophes and genocides all over the world. Does that stop her? No. Fuck everyone else, as long as it helps her career.

That's a female trait if I've ever heard one. Women constantly sell out their children and families lusting after the vaunted status of "career woman," which usually just means sitting behind a desk and shuffling papers in real estate. That's probably called equality in sewing circles and book clubs, but in my world it's called a dead-end job and a fucking waste of time.

Superman has only one weakness: kryptonite. Men are exactly the same, except that instead of kryptonite, it's anal. Women are just too stupid to think outside the box.

YOUNG MEN: BE MORE DICKISH

The children are our future, or at least that's what women say. Women are half right in this case, which is half more than usual. The children aren't our future. Young men are our future. Today's young men will be building the flying cars of tomorrow, and curing baldness in men and fatness in women just in the nick of time for me and you to enjoy.

Just look at what the young men of the past have grown up and done: They invented nuclear power, wrote and directed *Die Hard*, and built the Great Wall of China.

To give back to these young men for all their hard work, I've compiled a special section of wisdom in the following segment. I also want to educate young men about women so they stop sounding like such surprised jackasses every time a woman does something stupid. What were you expecting? Shows like *Ally McBeal* and *Futurama* feature female characters written by men who don't fuck up constantly like real-life women. Here's what to expect when working with women in the real world.

Repetition

The first thing to expect when working with women is repetition. When speaking to women, you are going to have to repeat yourself like a hundred fucking times with anything remotely important. Men hear something, remember it, and classify the information they heard as either bullshit, something funny, or something extremely important.

Talking to women is like snapping your fingers in front of a toddler's face to take a picture. Hope you have another roll of film in your man-bag.

If something is important, you have to say it to a woman three times in its entirety. Once so she can register who said it, again so she can figure out it's something to remember, and finally so she actually remembers it. You're better off doing it yourself, unless it's taking birth control pills.

Creative Fuckups

Even with your mighty man-brain, you cannot predict the ways in which women will fuck up. It's just like how you can't figure out the wrong answer to two plus two. Is it six? Is it airplane? Who fucking knows?

Sometimes a woman's fuckup is just marginally stupid, like repeating the same fuckup six times and expecting the last

one to work. Brilliant! But other times it's a real man-brain–
buster. How about a woman pouring an ink jet cartridge
into the part of the printer where the paper goes? That's a
pretty good one. Maybe she thinks printing reports is like
baking a cake? I don't know.

Or how about a woman addressing five hundred envelopes to your own office because she thought the return
address went in the middle. How in the fuck do you
get to be twenty-three and not know how envelopes are
addressed?

Conclusion

Always expect at least a half-dozen fuckups when dealing
with women in the workplace. This goes double if you're giving them something easy to do like show up at 8 or get you
a wake-up call at 9:30. Don't count on it. Unless it's stacking
paper plates or typing something that's already on another
piece of paper, do it yourself.

HOW TO GET LAID: DICK MASTERSON'S GUIDE TO LIFE

I'm not going to lie to you. When it comes to heterosexual
sex with women, there aren't a lot of alternatives to women.
However, women are easier to play than a musical greeting
card. They're just less pleasant to the ear.

Fake an Accent

It doesn't matter if you sound like the Swedish Fucking Chef, as long as you're saying, "Who's your daddy?" she'll eat it up like hog feed. Women are all inherently racist against their own race. Anything that looks or sounds different to what they know or have seen, is automatically their dream man. It doesn't even have to be a real accent. I once told a woman I was from Nairobi and I proved it by being unable to pronounce a *g* properly. I think I pronounced them like *f*'s.

Puppies and Kittens

Take stupid little animals with you everywhere—and I mean everywhere. If the bouncer at Pure won't take a twenty to let your guinea pig in, just slip a sugar glider in your pocket as a backup.

Sappy Songs

Women like flowers because flowers are completely worthless. They're just a bunch of wasted money. Women also love when you write them sappy love song lyrics on secret notes. Again, totally worthless. It doesn't take any time. They don't even have to be handwritten! You can just print some Bryan Adams songs off the Internet and slide it under her dorm room door. Slide it under a bunch of doors, who cares? You'll be getting laid within the hour. Just remember to write the directions to your place in crayon.

If you're an Internet guy, post all those shitty lyrics onto online personals. You'll get a bunch of fatties, but what did you expect? Women on the Internet are like a buffet. You can have as much as you want, and none of it's any good.

Manclusion

If you're nervous talking to girls, don't be. Just do what my friend Jeff does: imagine she's taking the biggest shit of her life. Jeff's a weird guy, but he gets laid constantly.

HOW TO NOT GET CAUGHT CHEATING

As a man, it's really up to you if any cheating is done in your relationship. Off the top of my head, I can think of about a thousand reasons why a man would be perfectly within his man-rights to cheat, such as maybe he's not getting it when and how he wants it.

Michael Jordan was caught cheating, and that is fucked. This is how you get away with cheating.

Dick's Way to Get Away with Cheating

1. **Shoot your personal details out of a cannon**

Personal details will always fuck you as a cheater. If you have a tattoo on your cock of a frog riding a motorcycle, there's a low probability of any other man having that and an even lower probability of a woman guessing it out of nowhere. Women don't know shit about math, but they know a lot about cocks. Any one of them could tell you those odds.

Once you've decided to start cheating, shoot your personal details out of a cannon. Put pictures of your cock on MySpace. That's what it's for, isn't it? A repository of pictures I don't want to fucking see, like fat seventeen-year-olds in halter tops?

2. Don't give a fuck about getting caught

Many years ago, I had a friend who was a shoplifter. We'll call him Alan Keys. What Alan taught me about shoplifting, I'm about to pass on to you.

Want to get away with something? Don't give a fuck about it.

I saw Alan walk out of a supermarket holding a watermelon above his head like the Stanley Cup. No one even bothered to stop him. If you're cheating, do the exact same thing. Take calls from the mystery lady during dinner. And don't hide those receipts! That looks suspicious as hell.

3. Constantly accuse your girlfriend of cheating

There's enough psychology on the back of a cereal box to teach you that constant accusations look suspicious. There's enough psychology for a man, anyway. Women don't think about anything. They don't think about consequences, they don't think about evidence, and they sure as fuck don't think about cereal. Cereal is delicious.

Women only react to things. If you accuse your woman of cheating, you just strapped a set of blinders on her and bought yourself a month of man-pleasing.

Also, only cheat with girls with the same color hair as

your girlfriend's. Or else come up with a really good fuck-ing reason why your shower is strewn with two-foot blond evidences.

FUCK MARRIAGE

This is perhaps the most important treatise in my entire book. It's also my favorite topic: marriage—and that it's stupid.

Do not get married.

Do not get married now. Do not get married later. Do not get married for looks. Do not get married for money. Do not get married for sex. Do not get married because people want you to. Do not get married because a woman wants you to. Do not get married because the Bible says to do it. Do not get married to have children. Do not get married for tax purposes. And especially, a reason more important than a brick to the head, do not get fucking married for love.

There are three main reasons why you should never get married, but in total there are three billion reasons: one for every woman on earth.

1. Marriage Is Against Your Manstincts

When in the whole universe has a man's *manstincts* been wrong about anything? I've seen a man punch through a wall three times in a row and not hit a stud. His *manstincts* were guiding him. *Manstincts* are accurate as shit. I've also seen a man win $30,000 at a blackjack table after his wife wanted them to go to bed. Guess who deserves none of that?

My cousin had a dog who wandered one hundred miles home from a stranger's house over the course of two weeks. That dog had a gender, and I don't think I have to tell you which one it was.

2. You Don't Have to Get Married

Have you ever seen one of those tags on the bottom of a mattress that says, "Do not remove this tag"? I've never seen one, but I've heard plenty of eighties comedians talk about them. How about one of those signs that says, "Do not fuck around on this grass"? Have you ever downed a fourth pint after a woman said you better not be doing just that?

What happened after you perpetrated that shit is exactly what happens when a woman threatens you over marriage and you do nothing: Absolutely nothing happens.

There was a part in *The Rock* when Nicolas Cage's hot girlfriend threatens him with a breakup if he doesn't propose. Scary, huh? She was pretty fucking hot. Well there was also a part in *The Rock* where Sean Connery had hair and the U.S. President didn't sound like a hillbilly. *The Rock* was a piece of fiction, fellows and gentlemen. Real women don't follow through on anything in their whole lives, including threats about marriage.

3. Plausible Deniability

If you go into a bank with a ski mask on and a gun in your

pocket, you're probably going to get stopped at the door. If you see someone in the middle of the street crack open a beer and drop their trousers, they're probably about to do something fucking stupid.

Getting married is walking right into a bank in the middle of the day with a beer in your hand and your pants in the street. Marriage is a binding contract and a passport to an imaginary, somehow nonsexist world where women have no earning power past thirty.

Don't get married until you can look yourself in the mirror and say this:

"*Hello, <your name said derisively>. Five years from now, I want to indefinitely support an adult woman out of pure benevolence and long after she has stopped fucking me, has probably started fucking as many other guys as possible, and always, always acts like a raging bitch to me for no reason.*"

You can't say that because you're a man. Marriage is for "lesbians," which do not even fucking exist.

DICK MASTERSON'S HOW TO GET A PRENUP SIGNED

I know I said my last article was the most important article in this book, but this one actually is. This is how to get a prenup signed. This article will save your life.

Step number one in getting a prenup signed is explaining to your fiancée what a prenuptial agreement is. While doing research for this book, I spoke with a dozen women about prenups, and I discovered something shocking: One out of two women doesn't know what a prenup is.

Actually, I wrote down all the results of the twelve women surveyed:

12 couldn't explain how to be "offside"

11 had never paid a cell phone bill

8 didn't know which way was north

6 didn't know what a prenup was

4 admitted to "knowing someone" who had an STD in her past

1 didn't have a cell phone

If she doesn't know what a prenup is, consider yourself lucky. Tell her it's an application to adopt twenty puppies after your wedding, or some equally stupid shit. Make it extra stupid for a laugh. You say "wedding" and she'll sign that fucker faster than she can pass out in your bridal suite.

If she's in the upper half of brainless, memorize the following and say it word for word. It will work. I guaran-fucking-tee it.

"<Her name>, I need to talk to you about something that's been bothering you lately — emotionally. It seems to me like you don't feel truly happy, and I want to make that right."

Great intro. First of all, it's guaranteed to be true. Women are never happy. Secondly, the best way to convince a woman to do anything is to show her just how fucking depressed she could be with the right attitude. Women obey like dogs when you give them that. Depression is a woman's bacon.

"You know why I love you so much, <stupid-ass nickname>? It's because emotions are so much more important in a relationship then silly things like making money and fixing problems. You're my emotional anchor. And I want to do everything I can to make sure you feel as emotionally supported as possible. Especially since we're going to be building a family."

I've disgusted myself with this jerk-off horseshit, so you men out there better use it.

"<Different stupid ass nickname>, I want you to know that I'm always going to be there for you—and only you. I don't want you to ever think I'm there because of the physical attraction we have, or the things we have in common, or even the kids we might share our lives with one day."

Now here comes the motherfucker:

"Or even something stupid like money. I want you to know in your heart that I'm there just for you and your feelings. That's why I think we should sign this love vow; a vow that says we'll be there for each other forever. I just need to know that I've done everything I can to make you feel safe."

And if that doesn't work, tell her you have like seventy grand in credit card debt. That's how you make debt an asset.

WHY WOMEN HATE SEX

Out of all the problems that have ever or will ever exist on the earth, there is only one that men haven't and will never be able to solve. It's unsolvable like a Rubik's Cube someone's fucking smashed to bits.

Women hate sex. That's the end-all, be-all of man-clusterfucks. But why? Women's sexual partners are the best lovers on earth. How could they hate sex? Human males are so good at sex, we invented love dolls just to stay on top of our game.

Do women hate sex because of some woman-guilt from an outdated, puritanical societal dogma? Or is it because women fear abandonment more than death?

Nope. Women hate sex because they're lousy at it.

Take a quick stroll down the checkout aisle at your local grocer's market. That place is thick to the rafters with women. In a manlier time, one might have called this the true department of Women's Studies. Take a look at some of the magazines. You'll find them steeped in a running theme:

"Ten Ways to Not Suck in Bed."

"Six Things to Do to Your Man that Aren't Lay There Like a Futon."

"Honestly, Who Gives Half a Fuck About Socks Being On or Off? That's Pathetic."

That's what women buy by the armful: guides on how to not suck in bed.

Women suck at sex like a wall sucks at playing tennis with you. You could be jamming around in bed like a maniac, pulling stunts out of your ass like Johnny Magic the Love Machine; maybe some whirl-arounds and body slams, whatever you want to be doing in the bedroom is your prerogative as a man, and that's no joke.

But it doesn't matter. A woman will remain unfazed and unimpressed, sitting there doing nothing, just like the wall, thinking she needs a new, expensive coat of lacquer.

In Chinese, the symbol for "crisis" is the same as "opportunity." I haven't looked that up, but I heard it from a man who had it as a tattoo. I assume he looked it up in advance, because men are better than women. What that symbol means for the Chinese, and for all men, is that during a crisis, we men are at our showstopping best. Take a flat tire on a moonless night, for instance. While a man is out changing nuts and bolts and doing all manner of work on the side of the road, will a woman so much as grab a flashlight to help? Good luck if you think she will.

Women hate holding flashlights, because they are complete rubbish at it—the same reason they hate sex. Force a woman to hold a flashlight, and you're likely to catch her aiming it into the sky for no goddamn reason. You're better off duct-taping it to a mailbox or just catapulting it into space.

EVERY WOMAN IS A CHEATING WHORE

I say it only because it's completely true. Flat out, every woman in the world is a cheater, has cheated, and is probably cheating at this very moment.

And is a whore.

Getting a woman to cheat on her husband or significant other is not like getting a woman to go to the gym. You get a woman to go to the gym by heaping shitloads of gifts and attention on her like a spoiled child and then ultimately getting no burn for your earn. In other words, no woman will ever go to the gym for any reason. Getting a woman to cheat is like getting a duck to eat bread crumbs. All you have to do is toss it in front of her face.

Getting attention from men is a woman's lifeblood.

Good attention, bad attention, the worst kind of attention; it doesn't matter to women. Being in a *Girls Gone Wild* video is just as laudable as serving in a highly respected public office. Women stack up eyeballs like empty pie plates at a N.O.W. convention.

A woman's lust for attention is like a man's desire to consume and waste things, two desires that are very manly indeed. Take throwing a sandwich in the street, for example. Do you know what's better than throwing a sandwich in the street? How about throwing two sandwiches in the street? Now, what if the second sandwich cost twice as much as the first? What if you had to wait in a huge line to get it? I would probably still do it, and I'm betting most men would, as well.

But what if that second sandwich cost you your dignity, your job, and your soul?

If we change "sandwiches" to "men" and replace "throwing them in the street" with "getting attention from them," we can easily draw the conclusion that women would do anything, and would stop at the destruction of nothing, for more.

Women think "cheating" requires a level of premeditation and malice on par with a fucking bank robbery. If the only evidence of infidelity you can produce is that she got drunk and put herself in a compromising position, you're up Argument Creek without a snowball's chance in hell. That means if a woman somehow convinces a coworker to "take advantage" of her, that doesn't count as cheating. It's just another horrible thing that's happened to poor, defenseless her.

It gets worse.

Women also don't count miring themselves in twisted, *Dynasty*-style emotional affairs as cheating. A woman may hang around with as many as five or six of her ex-boyfriends without batting an eye. She might accept niceties from male coworkers or university staff members without ever questioning the motives of a free back rub. That's a perfectly reasonable thing to be giving out, isn't it? A free back rub?

Bullshit.

WOMEN ARE DRIVING ME NUTS: PART I

When it comes to the simple task of driving—be it a car, a train, or a relationship into the ground—men are better than women. When a man drives, he is thinking of only three things: driving, not hitting things, and how to shave time off the clock. Women are completely the opposite.

When a woman drives, she is aware of only the fact that shortly after driving—after arriving at her destination—she will find herself among other people. People such as friends, family, and cashiers. As selfishly as possible, a woman begins to brainstorm the best way to extract a maximum amount of attention from her peers and superiors when she arrives at her destination.

That's what women are thinking about while they're driving. Fuck safety, fuck the rules of the road, fuck turning off the turn signal. A woman on the road is thinking about putting her makeup on in the car. Maybe if she does that, her friends will think her day is crowded with chores, activities, and martyrdom. Or she's thinking about how to spin a near-collision with a similarly out-of-control woman into a tale of panic and woe guaranteed to win her all kinds of delicious sympathy.

Women are addicted to sympathy like it's crack cocaine. They'll do anything for it, including driving down a perfectly straight road like a lopsided bowling ball.

DICK'S TOP TEN REASONS MEN ARE BETTER THAN WOMEN

I once sat down to write a list of all the ways men are better than women, but I accidentally crashed my computer because I filled up all the RAM.

So I did it again, except I opted for only the top ten

reasons. As a man, the moment I think of an idea, I set to work implementing it. It would have been exactly the same if my idea had been the wheel or the Hoover Dam. Men don't just take shit from the world around us. We dish it right back out.

Dick's Top Ten Reasons Men Are Better Than Women

10. Men do not have Tourette's Syndrome

I believe all women suffer from a mild form of Tourette's Syndrome. That's why they cannot shut their mouths for ten seconds, even while adults are speaking.

9. Men are not sheep

Women enter a situation and before you know it, they've completely changed their wardrobes and mannerisms as if they've joined a cult. Men are not sheep. Everyone knows the word for a female sheep is ewe, but what about the male word? There isn't one.

8. Women are hateful

Women's entire lives and social circles are based around hatred. Do they hate their boyfriends? Do they hate their wardrobes? Do they hate each other? Yes, yes, and fuck definitely. Men don't go in for that sort of womanly silliness. If we men are dissatisfied, we pick up and move out. Or we take our mighty man-muscles and lift a fucking mountain so the world looks exactly like we want it to look. Men do more world changing before 9:00 a.m. than any woman ever has done in her whole life.

7. Men live less than women

The last thing a society needs is a bunch of noncontributing members lying around and draining all the resources from the young. Men know this, so we blast off from birth like shooting man-stars—burning out ten years faster, but setting the whole night ablaze with manness. Women just kind of lie around like pigs in slop. Congratulations, women. You really earned those rights!

6. Men write illegibly

Writing is a stupid and ineffective way to communicate. Men know this, so we don't give a shit about handwriting things with hoops and loops and squiggles so big that aliens in space can read your notes about remembering to pick up your birth control pills.

5. Jesus was a man

Whether or not you believe in Jesus, there is one fact you can't argue with: Jesus was a man. No religion anywhere has ever put a woman in charge of shit.

4. Men wear watches

Do you know why men wear watches? It's because there's a limited amount of time in the day, and men need to know how much of it there is, so we can efficiently allocate our ass-kicking. Women don't wear watches, they wear bracelets. Like retarded kids in front of a taffy-pulling machine, women can just stare at a bracelet for hours and never get bored.

A watch says, "Get up and go! Move your man-ass and take care of your fucking man-business!" That's why *60 Minutes* uses a ticking watch for its theme song. "Important shit is going down and we're about to talk about it in a fastidious fucking manner, so get the fuck ready!" says a ticking watch. A bracelet says, "Look how much money a man spent on me!" What a joke.

3. Boys destroy things

The only thing that has ever lifted our species out of the trees from whence we came is our ability to destroy. Take paper, the cornerstone of the modern world. That was invented because a man wanted to beat trees into pulp. How about nuclear power? Men invented that by destroying atoms. Men are natural destructors. We pop right out of the womb and begin tearing down the earth with our mighty, manly man-fists.

Goddammit, that's awesome!

2. Marriage is stupid

Marriage is 100 percent the fault of women, but it was invented by men! Did you know that? Marriage was invented because women were too busy whoring it up to fuck the guy who was paying their rent and feeding their fat asses every day. Men invented marriage as a way of telling women who they could and couldn't fuck. Like everything else men have ever invented, it completely worked and worked way better than anyone thought. Women became so addicted to being told who they could and couldn't fuck that they now base their entire lives around it.

1. Men have penises

Having a penis—in other words, looking like a man and having man parts—is a man's way of telling everyone, "Hey. Look at me. I'm a man. I won't fuck up whatever it is that you're trying to do. If you need some help, ask me and I'll lend a man-hand. It's the least I could do to be fucking courteous."

WOMEN INVENTED TAXES

Two things in life are inevitable: death and women's fuck-ups.

Women invented taxes. I hate the shit out of taxes, because I'm a man and I don't like getting fucked blind-folded, mystery-date style. Let's take a look at all the precious things our tax dollars pay for.

Cops

Women are the only reason we need policemen—especially lady policemen. Women post their phone numbers on their MySpace pages, for fuck's sake. That's why we need cops.

If there were no women, there would be no violent crime. In a world of men, anyone walking around trying to steal shit or beat someone up would get his ass handed to him.

Taxes pay for the protection of women. I don't get why everyone says the Middle East has it backward. The women there can't walk outside without a man, but how is that any different than the way it is in America? Women here can't walk outside without a man, either. It's just that in our version, the man is wearing a badge, and at the end of the day he sends me the fucking bill.

Schools

I went to public school, and I had mostly women teachers. Women gravitate toward teaching because it's an easy job that requires no tangible results and deserves no respect—just like stripping. I can say for certain that on any given day, I bestow upon random children in the street more juicy gems of knowledge than any school will ever dispense with its publicly funded stable of she-donkeys. I say shit to kids and they say, "Wow, we never thought of it like that!" Teachers would murder each other for that kind of response, and I don't even have to try. I once taught some Mexican children how to read English, and I was completely drunk at the time—but that's another story.

Children respect men because we don't ingratiate ourselves to them like circus clowns. Without women, we would just send kids into the salt mines for their eighth birthday.

"Happy birthday, Asshole! Prepare to be educated."

Damn, that's manly.

Roads

Without women, the only cars available would be four-wheel drive. Lamborghinis would have tires wider than ten men and would reach top speeds of a thousand miles an hour.

WOMEN ARE OBSESSED WITH SEX!

Women say men are obsessed with sex, but that's bullshit.

Remember a time in history when women didn't trip all over themselves to be the first to talk about their precious dildo collection? It's getting to the point where just about anything can set them off on a ten-minute gush-fest about the best boyfriend they've ever had.

If anyone needed more proof that women were more obsessed with sex than men, the dildo is the nail in the coffin. How many men have fake women's asses at home? I don't know any. I also don't know any women who don't have a plastic penis stashed under their bed—one that they wish was actually theirs.

The seventies brought us the Equal Rights Amendment and the simultaneous squawking of billions of women all over the earth wallowing in "sexual reclamation" like a thousand-headed sow in a cesspool. A dildo is not sexual empowerment. It's proof that men are better than women at sex.

Women are so lazy, they actually need harnessed electricity itself to get their love motors running. The most a man has to put into a sex toy is fifty dollars for dinner and a movie.

IDENTIFYING A SLUT

Here's a fun *mantivity* you can do in your spare time. It's like homework, except you won't be graded on it. You're a man, so you already passed.

I'm asked the following question more frequently than any other:

"Dick, how can I tell if my girlfriend is a slut?"

The answer is as easy as your girlfriend.

Dick's Three Ways to Tell if a Woman Is a Slut

1. She has a cell phone

Women who are sluts always have a cell phone, sometimes two. Having a cell phone is the easiest way for a slut to garner herself a booster shot of attention, and attention is just a stone's throw away from sex.

Is tonight's free dinner not cutting it for the lady? Not a problem for the slut. She just whips out her cell phone during the entrée and cooks up a nice gumbo of drama and gossip with her best friends, whom she hates the fuck out of and for some reason can't wait forty minutes to call back. Even a hooker has enough class to turn off her cell phone.

2. She mentions another man

All sluts will mention at least one other man who isn't you during the course of a conversation. It could be a workmate, a neighbor, or a "friend," but if she's talking about a man, she's thinking about one thing and one thing only.

And yes, God is a man. If she's a church lady, odds are you have one hell of a slut on your hands! You lucky bastard, you know who to thank.

3. She wears heels

Everything about heels screams "slut." I'm not talking about the five-inch, Lucite, pole-dancer heels here either. I'm talking about pumps, boots, anything that isn't a regular sneaker shoe.

No matter what women say, there's only one reason to wear heels in today's society. She wants sexual attention as loud and clear and overt as possible. It's like a man wearing a helmet. Either he's expecting to be hit on the head at some point during the day, or he's retarded. It's the same with a woman in heels. Something's getting hit all right, and it's not her head. I'm talking about her vagina.

WOMEN ARE DRIVING ME NUTS: PART II

Women can't drive. And as usual I, Dick Masterson, have a whole trough of proof for your greedy man-snouts. This proof is so tight, it will lower your sperm count.

What do Liberace and women have in common?

They both love dick, and I'm not talking about me. I've never even met Liberace. I'm talking about having sex with men. Liberace obviously did it in a tasteful and subtle way, because he's a man, while women do it with velour pantsuits two sizes too small for their fat asses and with the words "booty" and "licious"—which aren't even words—embroidered across the broadside.

Liberace and women also both wear so many fucking rings that they can't drive for shit.

Remember those Looney Tunes episodes when Bugs Bunny dressed Elmer Fudd up as a woman? You know why that was so funny? Because Elmer Fudd is bald as fuck and pudgy and carries a shotgun. He doesn't look anything like a woman.

I laugh in the exact same way whenever I see a woman driving.

Fingernails the size of Fritos, platform sandals, a car ten times bigger than any woman has ever been able to handle. I could go on, and I will: ridiculously big sunglasses, fingers full of fucking rings, bangs in their eyes, breasts . . . How the fuck are women supposed to turn the steering wheel with those breasts getting in the way all the time? That's like a man trying to cross his legs or cry. We can't, because our balls get in the way.

Liberace could play a piano wearing two pounds of rings. Women can't even give a blow job after they get one ring.

DICK'S TOP TEN REASONS
GOING BALD IS MANLY

Going bald is like the menopause of being a man—so long as "increased chance of osteoporosis" actually means "increased chance of bagging a hot babe with your brand new convertible."

Dick's Top Ten Reasons Going Bald is Manly

10. Doing your hair is a loss of man-points!

And so is showering in the first place. The only time it's manly to care for your personal hygiene is when you're in a shitty wooden tub full of water and borax and you paid a quarter to soak for an hour, and it's 1855. Otherwise, you're losing about ten man-points a minute down your girly shower drain.

I took a one-and-a half-minute shower last week. That's got to be some kind of record.

9. Messy hair makes you look like a jackass

Have you ever seen one of those guys with a frizzy mop of hair sticking out his head? What are they called? Oh yeah, they're called teenagers. If there's one thing I know about teenagers, it's that most of them don't get laid and all the rest are liars. Sex doesn't occur unless there's a man involved. That's why all men are cool with bringing another girl into a sexual relationship. It doesn't count as cheating, because adding another appetizer to a meal doesn't make it two meals.

8. Accessories are womanly

Combs? Hair spray? Shampoo? These are silly, womanly things that must be fumbled around for. Anything a man touches should never be fumbled for. It should be revved like some kind of great mechanical beast, belching smoke and fuel out at incredible angles and forming a cyclone of poison around the wielder. Holy fuck, that's manly!

7. Bears are hairy

Men are not animals. We may be as tenacious as man-sharks and as powerful as locomotive rhinoceroses, but we're men. We're our own unique species of animal about a million times better than all of God's other crappy creatures. Being bald is like sticking it in the face of the whole lot of them.

6. Fuck Mother Nature

Just as it's manly to never ever wear a jacket for any reason, it's also manly to not have hair. Having hair is like bringing a jacket along "just in case." Jesus Christ, that's the womanliest thing in the world.

5. Sean Connery is bald

4. Bald = man smart

You know how in movies they always give some braniac with the cure for cancer or aliens this massive fucking hideous comb-over? That's because being bald makes you look smart.

One man looks smart because he spent a studious life toiling over the state of math and science, and he says and does smart things. Another man looks smart because he's bald.

3. Bald is badass

One bald man can kick the asses of six non-bald men. In the movies, any time a bald guy shows up, you know some serious fighting is about to transpire. Like how a cobra has a large set of eyes on the back of its neck to frighten away predators, the bald man can use his head to shine a reflection of his enemies' eyes right back at them.

2. Bald men remind everyone of The Penis

There is a feminist idea that says The Penis is a myth. The Penis is not a myth, and bald men are here to remind us of that. Just when you've forgotten about The Penis or just when some women gets it into her head that she might want to stop going to the gym and maybe eat another hors d'oeuvre before her salad arrives, in walks some bald guy with his giant penis-shaped head to set her straight—as straight as The Penis.

1. Bald is beautiful

Women will think and say whatever you tell them to think and say. If a women wants an apple and you hand her an orange, she'll fucking love it like it belonged to Jesus. Bald or not, you're a man, and you're in charge.

And someone tell Natalie Portman to put on a fucking wig. What's next? Is she going to start dating men half her age? Gross.

NICOLAS CAGE

Have you ever had sex with a woman who loved Nicolas Cage?
No, you haven't, because all women hate Nicolas Cage.

Nicolas Cage is so great, and he knows it. That's why
women hate him. He's also too manly for his own good, and
just like mustaches, and women hate anything that's too
manly for its own good. They can't resist throwing themselves wantonly at manliness for sexual gratification like sac-
rificial virgins—thus the hatred.

Nicolas Cage is so manly he changed his very own name
to more accurately match the ferocity of his manosity.

Can you imagine a world without *Face/Off* or *Con Air*
or *Gone in Sixty Seconds*? Of course you can, because you're
a man, but also of course you won't, for the same reason.
Men don't waste their days uselessly imagining horrible sce-
narios. That's why men don't make lousy, overprotective
mothers.

I was watching *Lord of War* the other day, and I arrived
at a frightening conclusion: Nicolas Cage is so manly that
everyone can go fuck themselves. Nicolas Cage knows no
mercy or compassion, and it's obvious in every move that he
makes. That's why his nose looks all fucking weird, because
he's like an eagle that's ten stories tall or a wrecking ball
with an indestructible spike welded to the side that makes
it look like a cool three-dimensional representation of the
man symbol. And that's just how manly his nose is.

Nicolas Cage had sex with his hot girlfriend on the roof

of a building during a conversation about how he's not going to marry her. That's the manliest thing anyone has ever done anywhere. The only way it could have been manlier was if the conversation had ended with a slap.

Nicolas Cage had sex with Angelina Jolie in a car he was in the middle of stealing. I saw *Mr. and Mrs. Smith* expecting that same kind of shit—I was disappointed. The fact is, besides Nicolas Cage and Jack Black, no man has ever told Angelina Jolie where she can shove it, despite how obviously she definitely fucking needs to.

Nicolas Cage delivered a monologue about how awesome and manly guns are while standing on a pile of spent machine gun shells. No one had ever done that nor will they ever, because spent machine gun shells are really fucking hot. Only Nicolas Cage is manly enough to stand on a big mountain of them. His feet are made of man-ice.

FUCK ORAL. AND ALSO ORGASMS

A properly inspired or inebriated man can learn just about anything he wants by watching television. It's like a font of information. Or rather, it's like a mirror and we men are the font of information. While watching television recently, I was reflected some statistics that I may well have known already.

70 percent of women have never had an orgasm during sex.

That's interesting, I thought. I would have guessed it was

way higher than that because really, who gives a shit about women and their fucking orgasms? No one besides whoever took that survey.

85 percent of men do not enjoy performing oral sex.

"Horseshit," I said when I saw it. The correct percentage is 100 percent.

If men were as bad as women at orgasming, there would only be like fifty people, and all of them would have headaches.

Men are in it for the species, sirs and gentlemen. Men don't let our personal problems and frigid attitudes get in the way of the species and our procreating it. That's something to be damn proud of. Letting personal problems get in their own way and also everyone else's way is the hallmark of Woman. For example, how many women have you seen crying at the workplace? Watch this, I'm a fucking mind reader and I'll guess your answer:

An inappropriate number, that's how many.

While they probably had good reasons for doing so, they probably also forgot that there is no good reason for crying in the fucking workplace. People are trying to get shit done and put food on their children's plates. No one cares if the boss was responding too well to your thinly-veiled sexual invitations or not responding enough.

A woman at work is a kitten stuck up a tree. She's got no clue how she got there, she's constantly crying for attention, and she's got no way to get up or down unless some man comes along and pities her. What a coincidence, that perfectly describes women in the bedroom, as well.

BITCHMAS AND HOW WOMEN INVENTED IT

Bitchmas is not a holiday *per se*. It is merely a name I, Dick Masterson, give to all holidays when they're ruined by women. Christmas, Halloween, Father's Day—you name it, women ruined it with their bitching, and they do so again each year.

I don't know why women have such a hard-on for wrecking holiday cheer and merriment, but they fucking do.

WOMEN RUINED CHRISTMAS

Women act like savages when Christmas rolls around. It's two months of screaming their heads off because some candle assortment isn't placed just right or because no one gives a shit about the lights. If Christmas lights are so great, then why don't we put them up inside the house? Because they're not great, they're cheap-looking and annoying.

WOMEN RUINED HALLOWEEN

Halloween is an excuse for women to dress like whores. That doesn't make Halloween special, that just makes every other day of the year unspecial. Why can't a slutty nurse costume also be pajamas in June? Because women ruined Halloween, that's why.

WOMEN RUINED VALENTINE'S DAY

Researchers estimate women will suck up approximately 13.7 billion dollars in Valentine's Day bullshit this year. That's 13.7 billion dollars in flowers, jewelry, and lingerie women will wear once because for some stupid reason women think lingerie is like soap: The more you use it, the faster it wears out. "You use it, you lose it" doesn't apply to lingerie, but it does apply to fat asses—way to get it completely backward!

According to some commercials I've seen, it costs just pennies a day to improve the lives of impoverished African children. "Just pennies a day" is a maximum of four pennies. If it cost five pennies a day to save starving African children, then they would just say "a nickel," because that's shorter to say and the saved commercial airtime could be turned into food.

13.7 billion dollars in Valentine's Day blood money divided by four pennies is 342 trillion starving African children. I don't need to check a globe to know there are fewer than that many starving African children in Africa. There aren't even that many starving African children in the whole world.

That princess you're buying a puppy for on Valentine's Day is taking a puppy's worth of meals out of the mouths of kids halfway across the world. And she loves every second of it.

WOMEN RUINED APRIL FOOL'S DAY

Women are the worst sports in history. If you want to go from "having a great day" to "completely embarrassed" in a fraction of a second, just pull a practical joke on a woman and get ready for a Fujiwara Force Five Hissy Fit. Hide the silverware before you do, unless you want your face pierced.

Women's souls are black and cheap and make them attribute all practical jokes to spite and malice, as they would have intended them. Also women have no self-esteem and assume anyone who's laughing is laughing at them, along with twenty other people who are going to hear the story later. They probably also think men masturbate to practical jokes. That doesn't make any sense to me, but it would make sense to a woman.

FATHER'S DAY IS A SCAM

Father's Day was invented by a woman who wanted to get a shitload of attention and praise for having the generosity to honor her father for one single day. If women are so interested in honoring their fathers, they would stop marrying such jackasses.

Men don't like to waste our time getting bent out of shape because of a bunch of nonsense. If you want to do something nice, then just do it. Don't make a big deal out of stopping off at Best Buy for a gift certificate and some discount James Bond DVDs after getting your nails done.

Men also don't set up obstacle courses just to watch the people they love trip all over themselves trying to complete insane balancing acts between "heartfelt" and "expensive enough." Women, on the other hand, invent holidays and anniversaries and then skulk around the calendar all year in the hopes that you'll miss one and make them martyrs.

THE WHOREY TRUTH BEHIND PLASTIC SURGERY

Some percentage of married women undergo elective cosmetic surgery.

I was going to look that exact percentage up, but I realized something.

There is only one way a woman can improve her marriage or relationship: morning blow jobs and more shut the fuck up. You might say, "Dick, that's actually two things, buddy." Well, unless you can introduce me to the first woman I've ever met who can shut the fuck up while not giving a blow job, it's one thing.

The real truth behind married women getting plastic surgery is that they are cheating whores.

Who is that boob job really for? The woman? Her imaginary self-esteem? Women don't have any self-esteem. Esteem is another word for respect, and self is another word for yourself. Would you respect yourself if you were a woman?

I'm amazed at the number of women who are on anti-depressants—amazed the number is so low! Antidepressants should be dispensed like M&M's out of quarter-turn candy machines in ladies' restrooms all across the world. Breast cancer donations haven't cured a fucking thing. Maybe it's time to donate to Dick's Xanax in the Ladies' Can Foundation.

Women have no self-esteem to improve. The only reason some percentage of married ones are getting plastic surgery is because they want more and more sexual attention from every man they meet. That's called cheating.

WOMEN ARE DRIVING ME NUTS: PART III

The most important part of driving safely is driving safely when you're drunk.

Look, it happens. You sometimes have to drive drunk no matter what, and women can just shut the fuck up about it, because they don't have to go pick up your car at 8:30 the next morning before it gets towed. They also don't have to work three and a half hours for free the following Monday to pay the impound fee.

If you think drunk driving is the eighth deadly sin or that drunk drivers should be thrown into prison for life, then stop reading right here. You're obviously a woman, and I've already said that you're not allowed to read this book. Women can only think one step at a time, but men think steps by the dozens or hundreds. We see great vistas of wisdom as we bound up the stairs of thought like we're running sideways. Go watch Oprah or do some finger painting.

Now, men, let's look at some numbers.

Of all fatal car crashes in 2004, twice as many intoxicated drivers were men.

Big fucking surprise. That's like saying a billion times as many deaths in wars have been men. Or that six times as many jockstrap-related injuries in 2001 happened to men. Women never do anything that might get them into trouble or ruin their precious images of themselves.

"I had no idea you were drunk when I got in the car!"

Yeah, right. It wasn't a clue when I stuck my head out the window and flew off the parking lot curb at forty miles an hour shouting, "Holy shit, I can't believe how fucking drunk I am while I'm fucking driving! Watch me spin out in the middle of the road! Yippie ki-yay, motherfucker!"

Sounds like I was pretty drunk to me. Women decide to let drunk men drive even when women are much more sober. That makes women the irresponsible jackasses here, not me, and not men.

Also, men can drink about infinity more than women while remaining better drivers. If they ever pass that law forcing drunk drivers to use red license plates, I'm going to go around every mall in the USA with a stack of red plates and a bolting gun. Every woman in the world should have one, sober.

THE MANLIEST MAN IN THE WORLD

The manliest man in the world is someone you've grown up with. He's a man you know very well. In fact, you've known him your entire life. This is a man who has seen his share of shit. He can be misunderstood, but one thing is for sure: when shit gets tough, he knows when to hold them and when to fold them. He's a fighter and a lover—sometimes both at the same time—and I'm fairly certain he would consider himself a jack-of-all-trades.

The manliest man in the world is: you.

You're a man, and that means you have a dick and balls. It also means you have that in common with every great historical figure who's ever done a fucking thing in his life. How awesome is that!

As a man, did you know that you have collectively fucked over thirty billion women? That's because you're a man and you share experiences, from Genghis Khan and Don Juan all the way down to Joe Schmoe. Some of those ladies were super hot, and for that you get a thousand man-points a piece. But some of them were ugly as shit, which gives you ten thousand man-points for being hilarious.

You're a man. You can't lose.

Have you ever seen a woman gloating over an engagement ring to her harpy friends? Disgusting. And women who agree with me and think it's disgusting are even more disgusting for selling out their own kind.

If it were the other way around and women had to buy

men engagement rings, then men would sell them immediately and buy beer for all their friends, because jewels are silly and stupid, except on Super Bowl rings.

Who abolished slavery? Men did. That means you did, because you're also a man.

Ask any feminist, and she'll tell you all men are responsible for the actions of their gender, and that means you're a violent rapist. But it also means you cured polio and you won the Strongman Competition for thirty years running. And you both killed and are Abraham Lincoln.

Man Zen.

MANCLUSION

You know, we've had a lot of fun together in this book. What we haven't had are any problems, because I forbade women from reading it. Sure, it'll hurt the sales. Women are voracious readers, because they're on permanent vacations and they can spend all fucking day reading and not lose a dime. But I don't have time to waste drawing pictures with construction paper and crayons.

At the end of the day, women are all special for some reason, even if we don't know what that reason could possibly be.

As much as women are special, they are also all guilty of everything I've charged them with in this book. Not most of them—all of them. There is not a single woman on earth who escapes mighty man-reasoning and flawless man-logic.

In conclusion, go forth and do whatever the fuck you want—just remember what I always say:

Don't get your nuts kicked.

—Dick

Appendix A: He Said, She Said

Part of your gift as a man is being gifted at things. Reading maps, balancing a checkbook, being taller than women, all of these things are part of the Man Equation of Greatness. The only thing women can be gifted at is having large breasts. Some of them have a great ass, but that's not really a talent because they'll fuck that up well before thirty. A true gift cannot be fucked up.

I, Dick Masterson, have a gift for putting my boot up the ass of women's accusatory, bullshit, straw man arguments. I should like to share it with all of you, especially you young men. The following rejoinders, when delivered properly and by a man, are guaranteed to shut women the fuck up.

Tear this page out and keep it with you. It will make you rich beyond your wildest imaginations.

DICK'S SNAPPY REJOINDER REFERENCE GUIDE

You wouldn't even be here if it weren't for women!
None of us would be here if it weren't for rape; does that
make it good?

Wasn't Hitler a man?
Wasn't Elvis?

You hate women!
Do you hate your old shoes because your new ones are
better?

Does your mother know you think like this?
Does your mother know you dress like this?

Being a mother is like having two jobs and they can't clock out!
They also can't clock in.

If you love men so much, why don't you go have sex with them!
Because they already like me for who I am.

Historically, women were never given the opportunity to excel!
Excellence doesn't need to be handed an opportunity.

Women are better than men at multitasking!
Fucking up several things at once is not multitasking.

Women are more emotional than men!
I hope no veterans hear you say that.

Men have caused all the wars ever!
Men have also ended them.

Men are only interested in one thing!
Football?
Sex!
Yes, but only when drinking, smoking, camping, movies, television, drugs, exercise, and merriment have been taken off the table.

Men are ugly and gross!
Here are some stamps and an envelope. Address that comment to: yourself in thirty years.

Appendix B: The Mantionary

There are terms in this book you men may know the definitions of instinctively, yet you have never read them or heard them before in your life.

That is because I have just invented them.

I find all languages at a loss for properly describing men and their greatness over all of God's other genders. Thus, I have taken it upon myself to invent the following words for my satisfaction. Manly of me, yes, but even more manly of me is to give their definitions without being asked to do so.

To those of you who keep insisting I call this the Dicktionary, let me ask you this: is America called Columbusville?

com·plete·ly mas·cu·line ku·dos

"Kudos" should never be said by any man ever, unless it's to tell other men that they should never ever say it.

Saying The K Word will result in a freefall, spiraling loss of man-points from which there may be no return. That is why I have devised a completely masculine version of the word that no man shall speak. I call it *completely masculine kudos*. When saying it, you are reinforcing the stigma of the original, while simultaneously promoting and bolstering yourself as a man. You are a pioneer of language, and you are letting everyone know that you don't take any kind of bullshit.

man·tas·tic

This is a word I use often, and for good reason. It's a word for those of us who would like to say that something is fantastic, but feel it's inadequate. "Fantastic" as a word has been tainted with effeminacy. It's a feminine word; it's got an *F* right there at the beginning. As such, it has lost all meaning over the years. What I have done here with *mantastic* is correct the mistake in the lexicon by putting a "man" at the front.

Use it sparingly, unless you can handle being goddamn manly all the time.

man·jo

Manjo is the shuck and jive of a man. It's the cut of his jib. More importantly, *manjo* is when a man moves and speaks in dazzling confusion, like a magician at children's

party, to keep women clueless and watching, slack-jawed, for
what's coming next.

Her: "Why can't I buy this purse? You bought a classic
GTO for $22,000 just last week."

He: "That's an investment."

Her: "Oh."

Now that's good *manjo*.

Man Zen

Men can hold many opposing forces within themselves
at the same time. Doing so is part of our lives from birth. For
example: Men have within them the mighty urge to punch
through a wall—even if that wall is not there. That's Man
Zen. A man could also think to himself, *Maybe I'm wrong,
even though I'm a man.* Could you imagine such a thing? This
ability to conflate wildly opposing thoughts is what guides a
man's spirit. It's his rambunctious impetuosity and his graceful wisdom and Socraticism.

That's Man Zen, motherfucker.

pe·nis·tor·y

Women get their granny panties in a twist about everything. Don't try and do anything right by them, because you
just fucking can't. One of their hot buttons is the inclusion
of "man" or "his" in everyday words such as "emancipate,"
"manual," and especially "history." If anything, "history"
isn't masculine enough! I had to read it like six times before I
even figured out they were talking about the "his" part.

Out of respect for the *Manculean* effort we males of the male species have been shoving into this great big shitbox of a planet over the last million years, I have changed the far-too-feminine word of "history" to the more accurate word "*penistory.*"

You can't fit "vagina" into any cool words like that, except *vaginopoly.*

man·pu·ni·ty

Sometimes shit needs to be gotten away with without a loss of your man-points.

Hugging with several slaps on the back is hugging that can be done with *manpunity*.

Also, when apologizing, if you ever say the words, "I'm sorry," you're groveling. That is not *manpunity* and is a major loss of man-points. Apologizing to someone who deserves an apology in the first place doesn't necessitate actually saying the words "I'm sorry." What's the point of that? Just to rub it in your face? You only have to realize you fucked up. Men don't need to hear apologies and women are always wrong, so fuck it.

Men are mind readers. How the fuck else could we get along with women for so many years? Women are the most retarded communicators on earth.

man·swer

Have you ever asked a man a question that he got wrong?

A *manswer* is an answer that a man isn't sure of. It's one of the many characteristics of men that make us a zillion times better than women. If you ask a woman something she doesn't know, she'll give you the most worthless answer in the world: "I don't know." Women would say that's called honesty, and they would do it in a crude and embarrassing way, but let me ask you this: If you ask ten men what Camembert is and nine of them say, "Some kind of Cadillac," does it make you wrong if you use it in that way?

No. It makes you a man.

man·mo·tion·al

Emotions are some of the manliest things in the universe. Last time I saw a guy break his fist punching the ass of a car, I thought to myself, "Damn, that guy sure is letting his *manmotions* get carried away."

man·stincts

Have you ever felt like someone was about to fuck with you? Or that you were about to fuck with someone?

When a man judges a situation or a person based on his gut feelings, that's called using his *manstincts*. When women do it, it's called racism.

Women's memories don't work the same way men's do. They actually work in reverse, so that a woman remembers what she wants to have happened based on how fucked up her current situation is. If she's pregnant, for example, and her husband is MIA, he will be remembered forever as the love of her life. It's that guy's *manstincts* that got him away from such a wacko.

man·tu·i·tion
See *manstincts.*

man·ti·vi·ties
A *mantivity* is anything that will net you man-points. Here is a brief list: drinking beer, making beer, pouring beer all over some hot babe, smuggling beer into places—anything with beer that isn't spilling it, basically—swearing in front of children, wearing sunglasses indoors, buying yourself presents for your birthday, sleeping in your clothes, continuing to drink after you've thrown up, throwing up after continuing to drink after you've thrown up, making out with some drunk chick after throwing up after continuing to drink after you've thrown up, arguing with a woman in an extremely condescending way.

man·joy·ment
Mantivities are *manjoyed.* They are never enjoyed, as that would not be masculine enough.

MNA
That stands for man-DNA. If God ever had sex with himself, then the male species was born of this union, and the blueprint for our mighty man-brains was encoded in our metaphysical *MNA.* That's some heavy philosophical shit that I just ended on.